Get a Grip on Your Lip

BETH JONES

Get a Grip on Your Lip
ISBN: 978-1-936314-11-9
Copyright © 2010 by Beth Jones

Published by Word & Spirit Books
PO Box 701403
Tulsa, OK 74170
www.wordandspiritbooks.com

TABLE OF CONTENTS

SPECIAL THANKS

I would like to give a special thank you to the following people:

Jeff, Meghan, Annie, Luke and Eric—Thanks for being the best family I could ask for. I love you with all my heart. Thank you for your faithful love and support and for allowing me to live on my computer during book-writing seasons.

Keith, Bill, Dave and Janie—Thanks for being a part of God's divine plan. I appreciate all of you. Thank you for believing in me and inviting me to be a part of the Word and Spirit team.

Joy Abad—Thank you for your fine and patient work editing. It's nice to work with a fellow Michigander.

Valley Family Church—Thanks for being the best congregation in the world. I love and appreciate you all. Thank you for your faith, prayers and support as I follow the Lord's calling.

The Lord—Thank You, Heavenly Father, Jesus my Lord, and Holy Spirit my Helper. I would know nothing, have nothing and be nothing if it were not for You. I pray You use this book to encourage Your people. May it bring You praise and glory.

Introduction

Words are powerful. They are loaded with the power of life and death.

When I think about the most significant life lessons I've ever learned, getting a grip on my lip is right up there at the top.

For many years, I got in trouble with my words. I'd swear, spout my opinions, be negative or say stupid sarcastic things. I would either say too much or too little. I often said the wrong things, or I put my foot in my mouth.

When I became a follower of Christ, I was still pretty clueless. I knew very little about what the Bible says concerning the words of my mouth, and I didn't know anything about the power of speaking faith-filled words.

Boy, was it eye-opening as I began to learn what the Lord thinks about my words. All it took was one reading through the whole book of Proverbs to realize I had a problem with my mouth. When I began to understand the power God has invested in my tongue, words, lips and mouth, it was life-altering. I started to be more intentional in the words I said or didn't say, and I saw remarkable results! The revelation and application of this subject has been a continual "aha! moment" for me, and I trust it will be the same for you too.

Perhaps through these pages I can encourage you as a friend, a sister, a teacher or a spiritual mom—plus as a minister—while sharing these simple yet profound truths I've learned about the power of our words from God's Word.

I truly believe the book you hold in your hands may be one of the most important things you'll read this year. I pray you dive into each page with a fresh expectation to hear from God and a passionate desire to put everything you learn into practice.

It's true, as the writer of James said, "no man can tame the tongue," (3:8). Without God's help, our words will get us into trouble, but with God's help, we can get a grip on our lip!

Happy reading and speaking!

CHAPTER 1

Sticks and Stones

Sticks and stones will break my bones, but words will never hurt me.

You know that's a big fat lie, right? Nothing could be further from the truth. Sticks and stones will break your bones, but words can break your heart, ruin your life and hurt others. Words are loaded.

The power of the words on our lips cannot be overestimated. In fact, the writer of Proverbs tells us really smart people teach their mouths:

> The heart of the wise teaches his mouth, and adds learning to his lips. Pleasant words are like a honeycomb, sweetness to the soul and health to the bones.
>
> Proverbs 16:23,24

In other words, wise people get a grip on their lip!

Get a Grip

Are you ready to get a grip and embark on a life-changing faith adventure? When you get a grip on your lip, your life will never be the same. Here's why: words carry the power of life and death. Words are power packed. They cut to the core or spread honey to the heart; they bless or curse. Words build up or tear down. Words bring forth great things, or they destroy our lives. Words frame our world. Words turn things around. Words direct our lives. Words set the rudder for the courses of our lives. Words start fires. Words ensnare. Words impart. Words bring joy. Words are seeds. Words produce fruit. Words are containers. Words are carriers. Words are not nebulous sound waves that dissipate into thin air; words can move mountains. Words play a huge role in determining our eternal destiny, the salvation of our souls and the quality of our lives on earth. Have you ever thought about the diverse power of words?

Let's bring it a little closer to home: have you thought about the power and influence of words in your own life? What types of things are you saying these days? What types of words have been spoken to you in the past?

When you think back to your childhood, do you remember any particular things that were said to you? On the playground? In class? At home? Perhaps sticks and stones *and words* have hurt and shaped the course of your life. Maybe you were surrounded by people who called you names or put you down with their words. On the other hand, perhaps you were fortunate enough to have people who encouraged you and planted seeds of greatness into the soil of your heart with their faith-filled words.

When you look at the current landscape of your life, what types of words are you speaking? Words of life or death? Words of hope and faith, or words of doom and gloom? Is your mouth bringing you joy or giving you fits? Is your mouth under or out of control? Do you find yourself saying things you hope people remember or things you hope they forget? Are your lips being controlled by the fruit of the Spirit with love, joy, peace, patience, kindness, goodness, faithfulness, gentleness and self-control; or are they being controlled by flesh, lust, anger, ego, selfishness, doubt, unbelief, strife and jealousy?

Getting a grip on your lip might be the single most important thing you do this year—or for the rest of your life. Perhaps the psalmist understood something about this topic when he prayed, "Set a guard over my mouth, O Lord; keep watch over the door of my lips," (Ps. 141:3 NIV).

It's true; words have the power to hurt us. But more importantly, words have the potential to help us.

Consider this rich tidbit from Proverbs, "The mouth of the righteous is a well of life," (Prov. 10:11). Imagine that. Our mouths have the potential to provide wells of life to our lives.

I am confident that as you get a hold of this huge biblical principle and put it into practice, you will see dramatic results. In fact, I have no doubt as the truths in this book become a part of your spiritual DNA and lifestyle, you will find yourself propelled into a completely new orbit for every area of your life.

Simple Word Truths

When I use the phrase "get a grip on your lip," I am talking about getting a grip on your mouth, tongue, speech, speaking, saying, talking, shouting, singing, confession, profession, voice, decrees, declarations, affirmations and words.

As we get started, let's take a bird's-eye look at several simple truths about the power of these things called words.

Words have the power of life and death.
(Prov. 18:21.)

Words have the power to bring sweetness to our souls. (Prov. 16:24.)

Words bring health to our bodies. (Prov. 16:24.)

Words produce fruit. (Prov. 12:14.)

Words can turn away anger. (Prov. 15:1.)

Words can stir up strife. (Prov. 15:1.)

Words can frame our world. (Heb. 11:3.)

Words snare us. (Prov. 6:2.)

Words take us places. (James 3:3,4.)

Words can make mountains jump and trees die. (Mark 11:20-24.)

Words bind the devil. (Matt. 16:19.)

Words loose God's power. (Matt. 16:19.)

Words make tremendous power available. (James 5:16.)

Words stop wind and waves. (Matt. 8:26.)

Words eradicate fevers and heal sick bodies. (Luke 4:38,39.)

Words give wisdom and kindness. (Prov. 31:26.)

Words teach. (Prov. 16:21.)

Words impart grace. (Eph. 4:29.)

Words bring us salvation. (Rom. 10:8,9.)

Words give wisdom. (Prov. 1:6.)

Words can please the Lord. (Prov. 15:26.)

Words affect us spirit, soul and body. (Prov. 16:24.)

Words feed people. (Prov. 10:21.)

Words turn away anger. (Prov. 15:1.)

Words make a way. (Matt. 3:3.)

Words disperse knowledge. (Prov. 15:7.)

Words provide favor with leaders. (Prov. 16:13.)

Words protect you. (Prov. 13:2.)

Words give joy. (Prov. 15:23.)

Words win favor. (Eccl. 10:12.)

Words are the language of faith. (2 Cor. 4:13.)

Words provide a well of life. (Prov. 10:11.)

Wise people teach their mouths. (Prov. 16:23.)

As you read this book, I hope you take some time to look up the verses of Scripture for yourself and allow the Lord to help you teach your mouth, guard your tongue and tap into the well of life. Let's begin our journey with words of prayer:

Father,

Thank You so much for Your Word. It is living and active. Your Word is Truth. I can trust every one of Your words. Thank You for giving me the unique privilege of being able to speak words that carry the power of life or death. As I begin this journey, I ask You to help me teach my mouth. I ask You for the spirit of wisdom and revelation as I read each page.

I thank You for the Holy Spirit, my Teacher. May I have ears to hear every word He speaks so my mouth may tap into the well of life You so freely promise. Thank You for helping me get a grip on my lip.

In Jesus' name.

Amen.

Words in Two Categories

Most believers know the importance and power of God's Word; that is, reading the Bible and listening to the Lord as He speaks to their hearts. Of course, His words are full of power: He's God! While most Christians know God's Word is full of life, many haven't given much thought or intentionality to the importance and power of their words.

God has a lot to say about the potential of our words. Let's look at the power of our words in two categories: words we say to or about others, and words we say in and by faith.

Words We Say to or About Others: The words we say to or about others matter. We can effectively build people up or tear people down with our words. Our words can impart grace to the hearers or pierce their hearts like an arrow.

Most of us know the types of words we should be speaking to and about others. We know we should be nice. We know our words should be kind and edifying. We know we shouldn't gossip. While we know these things, we all need a reminder from time to time to guard our hearts and mouths in relation to comments about others.

Words We Say in Faith: The words we say in and by faith matter. We have the God-given privilege of acknowledging, affirming, appropriating, confessing and laying claim to the riches of God's Word with words. As followers of Christ, we have been blessed and enriched by Him in countless ways; the more we declare by faith His Word in and over our lives, the more we experience the tangible reality of His goodness.

I love the way evangelical Christian leader Colin Urquhart of Kingdom Faith Ministries based in Sussex, England translates 1 Corinthians 1:5 in *The Truth New Testament:* "Because you live in Christ, you have been blessed with all of His riches. He has blessed you in every conceivable way. You know that all His riches are yours and you are able to speak His many blessings over your life."

Unfortunately, many people don't know who they are in Christ or how incredibly blessed they are as a result of being "in Him." Even fewer people understand the language of faith or the significance of speaking faith-filled words in and over their lives. They don't really understand the biblical principles or spiritual laws attached to words. For many reasons, they are unaware or misinformed about the potential their words have to move mountains and frame their worlds. They don't know what they don't know. As a result, some people have become confused, critical or dismissive about this topic and have thrown the baby out with the bathwater, as they say.

As believers, we need a fresh explanation of God's Word and the importance of speaking faith-filled words.

What does the Bible say about believing, speaking, affirming, declaring, decreeing, naming, claiming, confessing and professing God's Word? Thankfully, it says a lot. As believers, we need a fresh explanation of God's Word and the importance of speaking faith-filled words.

God Hears Our Words

Let's start with the basics. God hears our words. It sounds fundamental, but it is true—God listens. His ear is bent low, and He is listening to what we say. God's ears hear our words, and He's listening for some particular things. Before we look at all of the dynamics associated with our words, let's be reminded that God has ears, and He listens:

> "My voice You shall hear in the morning, O LORD; In the morning I will direct it to You, and I will look up."
>
> Psalm 5:3

> "I have called upon You, for You will hear me, O God; Incline Your ear to me, and hear my speech."
>
> Psalm 17:6

> "Hear my prayer, O God; Give ear to the words of my mouth."
>
> Psalm 54:2

Since God hears our words, we should listen to our words too. We should pay attention to what we say. Let's make sure we are speaking words the Lord can bless, use, prosper, maximize and fulfill.

Agree with God

A good place to start is by agreeing with God. Amos 3:3 says, "Can two walk together, unless they are agreed?" The answer is no, they can't. It's hard to walk together with someone when there is disagreement. We can't walk with God in a close, fruitful way if we are not in agreement with Him and His Word. Our agreement is made known by our words; our words are indicative of whether or not we are in agreement with God. If we want to walk in agreement with God, we must line our words up with His.

> If we want to walk in agreement with God, we must line our words up with His.

Think of it this way. God's Word is the plumb line—His Word is truth. His Word is settled. Our job is to listen to His Word and then speak the same thing, knowing He hears us. When we're in agreement with God, it's a lot easier to walk together with Him.

Have you ever noticed how difficult it is to walk with someone when they are in constant disagreement with you? Perhaps, if you're a parent, you know how difficult it is to walk together with your teenager when they challenge or contradict everything you say. Sometimes, we act like teenagers toward God, and our disagreeable, contradictory words make it impossible to walk with the Lord in the way He desires.

Inconsistent Words: The problem for many of us isn't necessarily 100 percent disagreement but rather inconsistent agreement. That is, our words bounce around all over the place. Some of our words agree with God and His Word, and some of our words contradict God and His Word. For example, one day we talk blessings, praise, faith, mercy, grace, love and positive agreement with the Lord;

and the next day we talk curses, unbelief, criticism, bitterness, anger and negativity; yet we expect God's blessing.

God hears our inconsistent words, but He cannot bless them. The Bible describes this type of inconsistency: "With our tongues we bless God our Father; with the same tongues we curse the very men and women he made in his image. Curses and blessings out of the same mouth! My friends, this can't go on," (James 3:9-11 MSG).

Harsh Words: In some cases, our words are full of harsh unbelief and doubt. Malachi 3:13-14 says:

"Your words have been harsh against Me," says the Lord, "Yet you say, 'What have we spoken against You?' You have said, 'It is useless to serve God; What profit is it that we have kept His ordinance?'"

The Lord listened to the words that were spoken. The Lord hears our harsh, stout words of disagreement.

When we say things like, "It's not worth it. God, what's taking so long? Why didn't You answer my prayer the way I wanted You to?" Or, "It's been useless to serve You. I sacrifice and tithe, and yet I see others who don't give a dime or lift a finger to help anyone but themselves, and their lives look so blessed; it's not fair!"

The Lord says, "I've heard you, but your words have been harsh against me."

When our words are harsh, we don't give God anything to work with. We need to eliminate harsh words against the Lord from our vocabulary. Listen, the Lord is your best friend. If there's anybody that's ever been on your side, it's God. He's your best, and maybe your only, friend. The Bible says, "If God is for us, who can be against us?" (Rom. 8:31). He has never had a day when He is not for you. So, while there may be some things you don't understand, you can rest in the fact that God has always been on your side.

When our words are harsh, we don't give God anything to work with.

Memorable Words: Did you know God is listening for memorable words? He's writing a book with some of our words:

> Then those who feared the Lord spoke to one another, and the Lord listened and heard them; So a book of remembrance was written before Him for those who fear the Lord and who meditate on His name.
>
> Malachi 3:16

Have you ever thought about this: God listens to our conversations about Him and records them. How would you like your words about the Lord to be recorded in the volumes of books in heaven's library?

It's true. God listens.

Words of Eternal Importance

Words are so important God has loaded them with the ability to impact eternity. The Lord is specifically tuning in to hear a few eternally important words from each and every one of us. The most important words we will ever utter have to do with our eternal salvation. Listen to what the Bible says, "If you confess with your mouth the Lord Jesus and believe in your heart that God has raised Him from the dead, you will be saved," (Rom. 10:8,9).

So, here's the million-dollar question. Are you saved? Do you know for sure when you die, you will spend eternity with God in heaven? Have you received the salvation Jesus has provided for you? It's as simple as humbling your heart before God, believing in Jesus and saying so with your mouth.

The passage in Romans goes on to say:

For with the heart one believes unto righteousness, and with the mouth confession is made unto salvation. For the Scripture says, "Whoever believes on Him will not be put to shame." For there is no distinction between Jew and Greek, for the same Lord over all is rich to all who call upon Him. For "whoever calls on the name of the Lord shall be saved."

Romans 10:10-13

Whoever calls on the name of the Lord shall be saved. God has given us the opportunity and free will to believe in Jesus from our hearts, and He's given us the power to confess our faith in His Lordship in our lives with our mouths. This belief and confession of faith is the very thing that will secure our salvation.

If you've never believed in, received or confessed Jesus Christ as your Lord, I can think of no better way to conclude my first chapter than to encourage you to pray this prayer out loud from your heart—and remember, the Lord is listening.

Dear God,

I am so glad You are listening. I want You to know I believe in my heart Jesus is Your Son, and I believe You raised Him from the dead. Today, I confess and say with my mouth, "Jesus, be the Lord of my life." I invite You to come into my heart, and I thank You for forgiving me of all my sins. I ask You to help me know You better and become the person You've called me to be. I believe it, and I declare it: from this day forward, Jesus Christ is my Lord.

In Jesus' name.

Amen.

CHAPTER 2

You've Got the Power

If you want power—real power—look no further than below your nose. Your words have power: "Death and life are in the power of the tongue, And those who love it will eat its fruit," (Prov. 18:21). Have you ever considered this reality?

God speaks words. We speak words. No other species has this ability. According to God, our words are loaded. In His sovereignty, the Lord has given human beings the ability to speak words, and He has endowed those words with the power of life or death. When you think about it, establishing this law of words among humans was a risky thing to do, yet it is quite remarkable that the Lord would empower His people in such a way.

The Law of Words

Throughout Scripture, we can see the power of God's words and the potential of our words. Let's take a closer look at this principle of words—what I will refer to as the law of words.

In God's kingdom, there are a variety of spiritual laws in operation. For example, the Bible describes the law of sowing and reaping. (Gal. 6:7-9.) This law works in a predictable fashion every time. In other words, this law of sowing and reaping, or seedtime and harvest, tells us we always reap what we sow after we sow; and we always reap more than we sow. If we plant good seeds into good ground, they will grow and produce fruit.

There are other kingdom laws: the law of faith, the law of the spirit of life in Christ, the law of love, the law of sin and death and so on. (Rom. 3:27; 8:2.) Each of these kingdom laws has predictable and reliable attributes. None of God's laws works in a vacuum; rather, His spiritual laws work in tandem with other biblical principles. In other words, the law of faith won't work effectively if separated from the law of love. The biblical principle of speaking faith-filled words does not work if it is separated from God's principles of wisdom. In God's kingdom, His principles overlap and complement one another. The spiritual kingdom laws are very much like natural physical laws.

Physical laws are working in tandem all around us, and it makes no difference whether we agree with the laws, like the laws or believe in the laws—they are working. It's in our best interest to learn about physical laws so we don't hurt ourselves and so we can benefit from them. For example, the law of gravity is a well-known law. The law of gravity works whether we believe in it or not. Our job is to cooperate with the law of gravity for our own enjoyment and safety. We can avoid danger, and we can experience flight if we learn how to cooperate with and maximize the law of gravity. Someone might say, "I don't believe in all that law of gravity stuff." It won't take but one leap off a tall building to make a believer out of him. That law of gravity will work whether he believes in it or not.

One of the spiritual laws we see at work in the Bible is the law of words. The law of words is working in our lives right now. It doesn't matter if we believe in it or not—it's working. It's in our best interest to learn about, cooperate with and maximize the law of words so we don't hurt ourselves and so we can benefit in the ways God intended.

It's in our best interest to learn about, cooperate with and maximize the law of words so we don't hurt ourselves and so we can benefit in the ways God intended.

Satisfied With Words

If you're looking for some satisfaction in life, put the law of words to work. Notice what Proverbs 18:20 says, "A man's stomach shall be satisfied from the fruit of his mouth." It's true. We eat the produce and fruit of the words we have spoken. If we were honest, we could look at the various compartments of our lives—our spiritual, mental, emotional, physical, relational, marital, ministerial and vocational lives—and see we are eating the fruit of words we have spoken. In fact, if the truth were known, we are where we are in life today in large part because of and as a result of our own words.

We are where we are in life today in large part because of and as a result of our own words.

So, how is your fruit? Are you satisfied with the fruit of your words? Let's look at a few practical ways this principle works in our lives.

Are you satisfied in your walk with God? Do you have a close relationship with the Lord? Does He speak to you from the Word? Is your spiritual life alive? Are you excited about sharing your faith and leading others to the Lord? If so, there's a good chance your words of faith have played a role. If you're feeling dissatisfied and distant from the Lord, you might want to consider what kind of words you have been saying. Have you been saying words like, "God never talks to me" or "when I read the Bible, I don't understand it" or "I don't feel God's presence" or "I'm not any good at sharing my faith"? The fruit of these words won't help to produce a satisfying experience with the Lord.

What about your mental, emotional or physical life? Are you satisfied with the fruit in those areas? Do you say things like, "I am strong and excited about life! I have the energy and mind of a person half my age"? If so, it's likely you're full of life and vitality. On the other hand, if you find yourself tired, sore and forgetful, have you heard yourself bring that fruit into being with words like, "I'm just so worn out these days"; "this old body is full of aches and pains"; or "I can't remember anything anymore"? If you've been saying these types of things, it's likely you are dissatisfied with the fruit of your words.

What about your relational fruit? What have you been saying about your relationships? Are you satisfied? Has your confession sounded like this: "I'm single and so lonely"; "I don't have any friends"; "nobody calls me"; "this person is so irritating, and that person is so boring"; "I am so mad at so-and-so" and "you can't trust anyone these days"? If so, you shouldn't be surprised by the relational funk and dysfunction in your life. You're eating the fruit.

Are you tasting good fruit or bad fruit in your marriage and family? What kind of words are you saying: "I don't know why I ever married him. My husband is a lazy bum," or "my wife is such a nag; I wish she'd leave me alone"? If so, you're producing rotten fruit and killing your marriage with words. Additionally, what are you saying about your kids: "My kids are so disrespectful. They just don't listen to me. These little monsters are running me ragged"? You don't want that fruit, do you? The fruit of rebellion and exhaustion will never satisfy you.

How's the fruit of your stability and success in life? If you've gotten in the habit of saying things like, "I am such a loser"; "I can't do anything right"; "I mess everything up"; "I am so depressed and scared"; "this world is a crazy place" and "I am just terrified of this and that," you will not be satisfied with the fruit of low self-esteem, anxiety, depression and failure.

On the other hand, if, throughout the years of your life you've said things like, "I am blessed"; "my marriage is strong"; "my kids are a blessing"; "the Lord is good to me"; "I can learn anything"; "I will succeed"; "I won't be defeated"; "I can do all things through Christ"; "the joy of the Lord is my strength"; "I know all things will work together for my good" and "God's favor surrounds me like a shield," you are likely eating the fruit of a consistently blessed, joyful and successful life.

I remember a season in my life when I heard myself saying, "I'm so stressed out. Everything is so stressful." I said this for several days, and then on the inside, I heard the Holy Spirit ask,

"Is that what you want?"

I knew what He was talking about. I realized what I was saying, and I didn't want that fruit. I immediately changed my tune. I asked the Lord for a phrase I could say that would produce the fruit I desired. As I pondered the busy season I was in, I remembered a phrase I had heard; it bubbled up in my heart, "Grace for the pace, grace for the pace!" That's exactly what I needed, so I began to say, "Thank You, Lord, for grace for the pace. Thank You, Lord, for grace for the pace." And guess what fruit I began to taste? Grace.

Fruit Inspection

Sometimes we're eating the fruit of words we weren't even aware we were saying. We mindlessly say things like, "Oh, this weather depresses me" or "my neighbor is driving me nuts" or "I hate my job," and then we find ourselves depressed, frustrated and unhappy. It's fruit.

A young couple that attends our church began to get a hold of these truths, and they made an agreement to hold each other accountable for their words. They wanted to eat good fruit, so they decided to be the "words police" for each other.

When they started, their ears were opened to their words. They heard themselves say, "That makes me sick," and "I'm so sick of this." Then they began to notice a pattern of sickness in their lives, so they made an adjustment with their words, and things turned around.

At another time, the wife noticed she was having a hard time standing in line at the grocery store or waiting for a table at a restaurant. Then she began to hear a pattern in her words, "I can't stand such and such," and "I can't stand that"; suddenly the dots connected for her. She quit saying those things and found her ability to literally stand improved.

On another occasion, she noticed she was more tearful and crying more often than usual. She didn't know if it was her hormones or what was going on. Then one day while she was at work, she heard herself say, "Oh, for crying out loud." She realized this was a phrase she said often, so she began to connect some more dots.

Of course, someone might think these are extreme, insignificant or coincidental things that don't make any difference, but then again if we end up eating the fruit of our words, perhaps these kinds of little phrases are worth considering.

We've all been guilty of saying phrases that seemed trivial—off the cuff comments like, "That just scares me to death"; "She drives me crazy"; "That kills me"; "That makes me sick to my stomach"; "You're killing me"; "I'm petrified"; "I'm just a worry wart"; "I can't remember anything anymore"; "I feel like nervous Nelly"; "That child of mine is gonna get himself killed"; "I'm losing my mind"; "She just about gave me a heart attack"; "I'm panic stricken"; "I'm so heartbroken" or "This economy is going to break me." These may seem like insignificant words, but the real test of their significance is in the fruit they produce.

Have you done a fruit inspection lately? Are you pleased with the fruit? Do you see a connection between words you've been saying and the fruit you are eating?

As you get a grip on your lip and speak words that carry the power of life, in due time, you will be satisfied with the fruit of your lips.

CHAPTER 3:

An Important Equation

Do you remember all those mathematical formulas and theorems you learned in high school and college? What about $E=mc^2$? Or the mathematical constant e, pi or the Pythagorean theorem $(a^2 + b^2 = c^2)$? Mathematical formulas, equations and theorems work the same every time. There's no second guessing, no hit or miss. You can count on it—E always equals mc^2.

In the same way, God's Word reveals spiritual constants as well— that is, things that are always true. Jesus gave us an example of this, "For out of the abundance of the heart the mouth speaks," (Matt. 12:34). It's a constant fact. Our mouths will always reveal what's in our hearts. We can count on it. Our mouths cannot speak anything other than what is in our hearts. If we want to change what comes out

If we want to change what comes out of our mouths, we must change what's in abundance in our hearts.

of our mouths, we must change what's in abundance in our hearts.

There is a huge heart and mouth constant we need to understand. If this were a mathematical formula, perhaps it would look like this: $m = h + a$. In other words, our mouth = our heart + its abundance. Our mouths are not independent—they are absolutely connected to our hearts.

When we understand this constant, we realize our ability to get a grip on our lip is actually a matter of the heart. To get a grip on our lip, we must start with our heart. So, before we go too much further in our study of words, let's talk about our heart.

The Heart-Overflow Factor

Jesus said, "For out of the abundance of the heart the mouth speaks," (Matt. 12:34). There is no question where words come from. Jesus said words come out of the abundance of the heart. In other words, our speech reveals what we really believe in our hearts. It's easy to tell what's in our hearts; we just need to listen to what we say.

For example, if you have an abundance of sports in your heart, then sports will come out of your mouth. No one has to pull it out of you. Sports will come out. Why? If sports fill your heart, sports will fill your mouth.

If you have abundant bitterness or self-pity in your heart, nobody has to pull it out of you. Everything you say is just going to sound bitter or pitiful because that is what fills your heart.

On the positive side, if you want kindness to come out of your mouth, you have to fill your heart with mercy, grace, love, patience and kindness. If you want godly wisdom to come out of your mouth, you have to fill your heart with God's Word, godly knowledge, understanding, discernment and discretion. Whatever fills your heart in abundance is what will come out of your mouth. This is a constant.

Now, it gets even more interesting. Proverbs tells us the power of life and death is in our tongues. (Prov. 18:21.) That is, whatever comes out of our mouths has the power of life or death. So, if we want life to pour forth from our tongue, we must be certain that life fills our hearts. The only way to guarantee we experience life is to be certain life comes out of our mouths—and the only way to be certain this happens is to make sure life fills our hearts in abundance. Get the idea?

If we're having trouble with our lips, the place to fix it is in our hearts. We have to load our hearts with the things we want to experience in life because our mouths will automatically speak from the abundance in

We can't discipline ourselves enough to tame the tongue; but if we will fill our hearts with the right things, our mouths will speak out of the abundance of our hearts.

our hearts, and the words we say will produce either life or death. Trying to exercise self-discipline with our tongues won't do it. In fact, I am not suggesting people strain to have self-control over their mouths. It's not possible to do unless there is a change of heart-content. We can't discipline ourselves enough to tame the tongue; but if we will fill our hearts with the right things, our mouths will speak out of the abundance of our hearts.

The secret to controlling our mouths is our hearts.

More Than Positive Words

The idea of getting a grip on our lip is more than speaking positive words and using the power of positive thinking. Speaking faith-filled words is not just a matter of having positive speech or following metaphysical theories or new-age ideas—it's much more than that. The secular world's belief in the Pygmalion effect (i.e., self-fulfilling prophecies and the power of positive statements) is man's attempt at creating counterfeits of a genuine, godly, biblical principle. The law of words is not a matter of coming up with magical phrases, passwords, formulas, humanistic words of affirmation or sentences that work like a charm.

God's principles of faith and speaking power-packed words are based upon His Word. Living by the law of words is a way of life, not a magic bullet, new program or special event. To get a grip on your lip is to live a lifestyle where out of the abundance of your heart, you speak faith-filled words congruent with God's Word and His will.

Let's continue to look at what He says about this topic.

Bring Forth Good Things

Do you want to bring forth good things in your life? Here's what Jesus said:

> "Either make the tree good and its fruit good, or else make the tree bad and its fruit bad; for a tree is known by its fruit. Brood of vipers! How can you, being evil, speak good things? For out of the abundance of the heart the mouth speaks. A good man out of the good treasure of his heart brings forth good things, and an evil man out of the evil treasure brings forth evil things. But I say to you that for every idle word men may speak, they will give account of it in the day of judgment. For by your words you will be justified, and by your words you will be condemned."
>
> Matthew 12:33-37

In this passage, notice the phrase "brings forth." How do we bring forth things from the treasure of our hearts? We bring forth things through the words we speak: "A good man out of the good treasure of his heart brings forth good things." On the contrary, "An evil man, out of the evil treasure, brings forth evil things." How does that happen?

By the words he speaks. The way we bring forth good or evil is through the words we speak from the abundance that fills our hearts. This is the law of words in operation.

So then if our spiritual calculations, formulas, theorems and equations are correct, and if we want to get a grip on our lips, we need to spend time meditating, soaking, saturating and marinating our hearts in God's Word. When we let the Word of Christ dwell in us richly (Col. 3:16), we will fill our hearts with an abundance of good things; out of the abundance of our hearts, our mouths will speak.

When I was very new Christian, I didn't know anything about spiritual constants, biblical principles or the law of words; thankfully, the Holy Spirit did, and He began to teach me the power of putting God's Word in my mouth.

As a thirteen year old and the oldest daughter of four girls, when my parents divorced, I felt an extra responsibility to protect my sisters and help my mother. Somewhere along the way, without a father in the house and being raised by a single mother, I developed a bit of a rejection complex. I didn't realize it at the time, and I didn't know God wanted to change it, but He went to work filling my heart with His Word regarding His favor and approval.

One day, as I was reading the Bible, Psalm 5:12 NIV seemed to leap off the page: "For surely, O Lord, you bless the righteous; you surround them with your favor as with a shield."

I was especially drawn to the phrase, "You surround them with your favor as with a shield." I started to repeat this phrase daily. I would say,

"Thank You, Lord. You surround me with favor as with a shield. Everywhere I go, people like me; and I have good relationships with people. Thank You for special favors and advantages."

Guess what happened? I noticed God's favor and blessings surrounded me everywhere I went, and I enjoyed favorable relationships. I realized God's favor had been brought forth because I got my words in agreement with His Word.

As you purpose to fill your heart with God's Word, from the abundance of your heart, you will speak; and over time you will bring forth good things.

Are you ready to fill your heart with the good things of God's Word so you can bring them forth with the words of your mouth? As you purpose to fill your heart with God's Word, from the abundance of your heart, you will speak; and over time you will bring forth good things.

The psalmist David must have had some revelation on this subject when he prayed,

"Let the words of my mouth and the meditation of my heart be acceptable in Your sight, O Lord, my strength and my Redeemer."

(Psalm 19:14).

CHAPTER 4

Killing Me Softly

Have you noticed the divisive verbal climate, negative tone and polarizing speech in our culture? Instead of carefully choosing our words or guarding our mouths, many people in our society are loose with their lips and bringing forth evil things with their words. The unfortunate result is the law of words has gone to work in a way that has been detrimental to individuals, families, communities, churches, organizations, cities, states and nations. We have been snared with our words. Roberta Flack may have had it right when she sang, "Killing me softly with his words, killing me softly."

Snared by Words

As we have seen, words are powerful; yet left unchecked, words can imprison us. Words trap us. Words snare us. Proverbs 6:2 says:

"You are snared by the words of your mouth; You are taken by the words of your mouth."

As I look back, in my own life, I can see areas where I snared myself with my own words. One memorable trap I found myself in had to do with getting the flu. Over the course of a couple of annual Thanksgiving celebrations, I noticed I came down with a 24-hour stomach flu. As a result, I started to say, "I always get the flu around Thanksgiving." And, sure enough, for several years, I got a 24-hour stomach flu sometime before or after Thanksgiving. This happened year after year. I expected the flu. I prepared for the flu. I declared the flu and . . . I got the flu!

After I came to Christ and began to learn God's Word, I realized I had snared myself with my own words. Eventually, I learned about the power of life and death in my tongue, so I began to say what God says about my health and wellness. I got a hold of Psalm 103, and I began to say things like, "I don't get the flu around Thanksgiving because Jesus is my Lord and Healer. He has forgiven me of all my sins and healed me of all my diseases."

I changed my tune, and guess what happened? I didn't get the flu around Thanksgiving that year or the year after that or the year after that. I can't tell you the last time I had the flu, but I can guarantee you it wasn't around Thanksgiving. Why? Because I don't get the flu around Thanksgiving.

This was a simple but powerful lesson for me.

If we don't want to be snared by our words, we will have to eliminate some things from our vocabulary. We can't continue to say, "I always get sick"; "I can't do that";

"I'm not good at anything"; "I don't know how I'm gonna pay my bills"; "with my luck, my car will probably break down"; "I'm such an idiot"; "I'm depressed" or the like. We can't say, "I'll never have nice things" or "I could never afford a house like that" or "we could never take a vacation like that" or "I could never go to college or get a high-paying job." Don't put yourself in a trap with your words.

Get God's Word in your mouth, and begin to declare what He says about who you are and what you can have. If God has promised you something in His Word, don't contradict Him. If He says He meets all your needs according to His glorious riches in Christ, believe Him and speak the same. (Phil. 4:19.) If He says delight yourself in the Lord, and He'll give you the desires of your heart (Ps. 37:4), agree with Him and speak it.

When my husband and I were newlyweds, we enjoyed going for walks through the really nice neighborhoods in our town. Some of the homes were mansions, and we would say to one another, "Who lives in a house like that?" On a few occasions we said things like, "I can't imagine living in a house like that" or "this must be how rich people live."

By our words, we were implying we weren't those rich people and we never would be. We were developing faith in our inability to have a nice home. The Lord corrected us, and we quit saying those things. Instead of trapping ourselves by confessing what we didn't have, we put

God's Word in our mouths, and we declared both His Word and our desires regarding our future homes.

Have you been snared by any of your words? If so, I have good news for you. Though certain words may have snared or trapped you, faith-filled words can spring you free. If your words have gotten you into a mess, be encouraged in knowing your words can play a role in getting you out of that mess.

Higher Heights or Down the Tubes?

Are your words taking you to higher heights or down the tubes?

Like many states, Michigan's economy has had its ups and downs. Throughout the cycle, I've observed an interesting phenomenon. Those who cooperate with God—that is, operating in His wisdom, being led by the Spirit and employing the law of words—survive and prosper; while those who don't cooperate with the Lord and His ways tend to struggle or go broke.

In every economic upturn or downturn, someone is making money. Everyone isn't going bankrupt. Some people are succeeding, so it might as well be you. If you will be led by the Holy Spirit and cooperate with God, His Word, His wisdom and His kingdom laws, you can expect a good outcome.

Years ago I knew a man who started a new business with a novel approach. He launched out on a faith adventure with dreams of making it big. He was a young Christian, full of vision and zeal and unfortunately, just enough knowledge of God's Word to be dangerous . . . to himself.

He was full of faith as he launched his new business. He spoke God's blessings and success over his business. At first everything went well. Then he hit a slump. The economy dipped, and the novelty of his business waned. Instead of staying strong, trusting the Lord and intentionally putting God's Word and the law of words to work in a positive way, he got discouraged and began to ensnare himself with his own words.

Day after day he said, "I'm going down the tubes. I am taking a slow boat to China, and my business is going down the tubes." Day after day his business got worse. Customers quit coming. He had to let employees go, and in a short time, guess what happened? He went down the tubes: he went bankrupt. The unfortunate thing is he never really understood true Bible faith nor the law of words working against him. Instead, he blamed God for his failure, and it took years for him to recover spiritually and financially.

Obviously, there is more to running a successful business than just speaking faith-filled words. Any business owner needs to operate in wisdom, integrity, innovation and good business practices in addition to being led by the Holy Spirit and activating the supernatural element of faith and words. At the same time, the worst thing for business people to do is add insult to injury by ensnaring themselves with their words when their businesses are facing a setback.

If you've been snared and trapped by your words, take some time to meditate on God's Word and allow it to bring correction.

"Do you see a man who is hasty in his words? There is more hope for a [self-confident] fool than for him."

Proverbs 29:20 AMP

"A [self-confident] fool's lips bring contention, and his mouth invites a beating. A [self-confident] fool's mouth is his ruin, and his lips are a snare to himself."

Proverbs 18:6,7 AMP

"The words of a wise person are gracious. The talk of a fool self-destructs—He starts out talking nonsense and ends up spouting insanity and evil. Fools talk way too much, chattering stuff they know nothing about."

Ecclesiastes 10:12-14 MSG

Good Traps

While we can be trapped by our words—in a negative way—on the positive side, we can trap ourselves with words into some good things. How would you like to be trapped in good things by good words?

My husband and I have been trapping our kids with words for years. From the time they were infants, we've said intentional words to trap them in love, peace, joy and success. We intentionally chose nicknames that would bring forth good things. We called one of our kids "Sunshine," and another one we nicknamed "Super-Sweet-Smiler Boy." We did this to free them from any moody, grumpy traps lying around.

When our kids started school, we proactively set a trap of security and protection by engaging our kids with positive words before they went to school each day. We would begin by asking them, "What do you know?"

Then we coached them to respond with these words, "God loves me. Jesus loves me. Mom loves me. Dad loves me. Meghan loves me. Annie loves me. Luke loves me. Eric loves me. I love myself. I'm a good friend, and I'm going to have a great day."

Once they said those words, we would say, "Okay, the name of Jesus, the blood of Jesus and the angels of God surround and protect you, take you to school safely, keep you at school safely and bring you home from school safely. You love to learn. You have the mind of Christ. You're a good friend to your friends. You're a leader, and today's going to be a _____ day!" (We would fill in the blank with a variety of descriptive words—a great day, a day of laughter, a day of leadership, a day of favor, a day of peace, etc. Whatever seemed fitting for that day, we'd say it.)

Why did we say these things to our kids every day? We wanted to ensnare them with our words. We wanted them trapped in God's love.

We've done the same thing in our own lives. We intentionally declare God's Word and say these kinds of faith-filled words of protection when we get on an airplane, take a long trip, go skiing, ride motorcycles or do just about anything. What are we doing? We are trapping ourselves with good words. We are snared by our words.

Acknowledgement Received

Another way we can trap ourselves in God's goodness is by acknowledging the good things that belong to us in Christ.

> I thank my God, making mention of you always in my prayers, hearing of your love and faith which you have toward the Lord Jesus and toward all the saints, that the sharing of your faith may become effective by the acknowledgment of every good thing which is in you in Christ Jesus.
>
> Philemon 1:4-6

Have you ever been acknowledged? Has someone acknowledged your hard work? Your great attitude? Your sacrifice? Have you ever been acknowledged for your kindness? Generosity? Leadership? How did it feel to be acknowledged?

No doubt about it—it made the person who acknowledged things a bit more effective in your mind and heart.

Have you ever made an effective communication—perhaps online or at the ATM—and after the transaction was complete, you received a notice that said, "Acknowledgment received"?

There is a strong parallel in our Christian lives: if we want to experience effective transactions with God and others, we must acknowledge things. In Philemon 1:6, the word *acknowledge* denotes: "exact or full knowledge, discernment, recognition," and "a greater participation by the 'knower' in the object 'known,' thus more powerfully influencing him." Another biblical dictionary defines it as "to admit the existence, reality, or truth of; to recognize as being valid or having force or power; to express recognition of; to express thanks or gratitude for; to report the receipt of and to accept or certify as legally binding."

When we acknowledge—have an exact knowledge of, a greater participation in, recognize, verbalize, admit, express thanks for, accept and certify—the good things God has done in and for us because we are in Christ, we will discover our faith is more effective. Which types of good things do we need to acknowledge? Acknowledge "every good thing which is in you in Christ," (Philemon 1:6).

Here's a partial list of the good things we need to recognize and verbalize. When we acknowledge these good things by saying them out loud, we trap ourselves in our identity in Christ.

I am the righteousness of God—in Christ. (2 Cor. 5:21.)

I am more than a conqueror—in Christ. (Rom. 8:37.)

I can do all things—through Christ. (Phil. 4:13.)

I am an ambassador—for Christ. (2 Cor. 5:20.)

I am accepted—in Christ. (Eph. 1:6.)

I am forgiven—in Christ. (Col. 2:13.)

I am a new person—in Christ. (2 Cor. 5:17.)

I am healed—in Christ. (1 Pet. 2:24.)

I am free—in Christ. (Gal. 5:1.)

I am filled with peace—in Christ. (Phil. 4:7.)

I am blessed with every spiritual blessing—
in Christ. (Eph. 1:3.)

I am an overcomer—in Christ. (1 John 5:4,5.)

I am seated in heavenly places—in Christ.
(Eph. 2:6.)

I am redeemed—in Christ. (Gal. 3:13.)

I am triumphant—in Christ. (2 Cor. 2:14.)

I am victorious—in Christ. (1 Cor. 15:57.)

I am filled with wisdom—in Christ. (1 Cor. 1:30.)

I am saved and called—in Christ. (2 Tim. 1:9.)

What kinds of traps are you setting? Instead of being snared by negative words, go ahead and trap yourself by speaking God's Word. As you acknowledge God's Word in your life on a regular basis, you will find yourself trapped in the victorious, joyful, fruit-bearing Christian life.

CHAPTER 5:

Move That Mountain

Ever talked to a tree? How about a mountain? A fever? The wind? Big waves? Jesus did. Then He had the audacity to tell others they could do the same thing: "Jesus answered and said to them, 'Have faith in God. For assuredly, I say to you, whoever says to this mountain, "Be removed and be cast into the sea," and does not doubt in his heart, but believes that those things he says will be done, he will have whatever he says,'" (Mark 11:22,23).

Have you talked to any "thing" lately? Shortly after our church did a series on this topic, we received this testimony from one of the women in attendance:

My husband had been laid off of work for months and months. Last week my husband called his employer for the weekly disappointment of "no work yet." We went to church on Saturday, and we heard the message on the power of God's Word in our mouths. We desperately needed God's financial favor, so we went home and made a pact that the two of us were going to agree with God and speak it out loud.

Last night, my husband received the call that he could go back to work today! He had been laid off for eight weeks, so we needed this. Through our faith in God, He prevailed.

This family took Jesus at His Word and saw wonderful results!

These Lips Were Made for Talking

Jesus taught us our lips were made for talking: look at the whole story in Mark 11.

Jesus has just made a triumphal entry into Jerusalem, and he enters the temple. When the hour grows late, He and his disciples leave the city and go to Bethany for the night. The next day, as Jesus is leaving Bethany and heading back to Jerusalem, He teaches his disciples (and us) a lesson about the power of faith and words.

The next day, when they come out from Bethany, He is hungry. Seeing from afar a fig tree having leaves, He goes to see if perhaps He could find something on it. When He comes to it, He finds nothing but leaves, for it is not the season for figs. In response, Jesus says to it, "Let no one eat fruit from you ever again," and His disciples hear it. (Mark 11:12-14.)

Jesus was hungry, so He looked for figs on a nearby tree. The tree did not have any fruit, and Jesus responded by talking to the fig tree. Did you catch that? Jesus talked to a tree, and apparently the tree heard Him. Not only that, He spoke loudly enough that His disciples heard it. The story continues:

Now in the morning, as they passed by, they saw the fig tree dried up from the roots. And Peter, remembering, said to Him, "Rabbi, look! The fig tree which You cursed has withered away."

So Jesus answered and said to them, "Have faith in God. For assuredly, I say to you, whoever says to this mountain, 'Be removed and be cast into the sea,' and does not doubt in his heart, but believes that those things he says will be done, he will have whatever he says. Therefore I say to you, whatever things you ask when you pray, believe that you receive them, and you will have them."

Mark 11:20-24

Let's summarize the situation. Jesus walked by a fig tree and noticed that the tree was not producing fruit. Jesus spoke to the fig tree and said, "Let no one eat fruit from you ever again." The next day, the disciples walked by it and saw the tree was dried up from the roots. The fig tree heard and obeyed Jesus' words.

It's one thing for Jesus to speak to trees—to declare words that carry life and death. After all, He is God. Jesus often talked to things. He talked to trees, wind and waves. He rebuked a fever that afflicted Peter's mother-in-law, and she was healed. Jesus talked to things, and, apparently, these things heard Him. This should not surprise us; we would expect His words to have authority and power, right?

However, it's another thing for human beings to talk to things. Nevertheless, as the story continues, Jesus does something remarkable—He tells us to talk to things. He delegates the authority and responsibility for talking to things to whomever. Jesus tells all the whomevers they can talk to things. In fact, Jesus commands it. He tells us to have faith in God, and then He follows up that statement by instructing us to speak in the same way He spoke to the fig tree. All of us can speak to the mountains in our lives.

If you are a whoever, your lips were made for talking. Let's take a closer look at what Jesus said.

Jesus Told Us to Open Our Mouths

"Have faith in God. For assuredly, I say to you, whoever says to this mountain, 'Be removed and be cast into the sea,' and does not doubt in his heart, but believes that those things he says will be done, he will have whatever he says," (Mark 11:22,23).

After Jesus spoke to the fig tree, He told us to follow His example by having faith in God and speaking to mountains. Notice, Jesus said, "Have faith in God." In

Young's Literal Translation, verse twenty-two reads this way, "And Jesus answering saith to them, 'Have faith of God.'" In other words, He tells us to have the same type of faith God has—the same type of faith He had when speaking to the fig tree.

Jesus went on to say, "Whoever of you says to this mountain. . . . " Notice, He said the God-kind of faith is available for whomever. That means every believer is qualified to have the faith of God and speak to mountains. If we want our mountains to move, we will have to open our mouths and start talking.

If you carefully study Mark 11:23, you will see that while having faith in God is important, Jesus mentioned the importance of what we say three times while He only mentioned what we believe once. Jesus is emphasizing your need for speaking faith-filled words when you face mountains.

Notice that Jesus *didn't* say, "Hey followers, don't you dare try this. I'm Jesus—God in the flesh—I talk to trees, but you shouldn't try this. You can't have this kind of faith. Just leave all the talking to Me."

If Jesus didn't intend for His followers to follow His example of speaking to things, this would have been the perfect time to set the record straight. This would have been the opportune time for Him to let the disciples know it would be presumptuous, arrogant and out of line for them—or whomever—to think they could speak words of power to mountains.

Instead, Jesus did the exact opposite. He took this occasion to advise, empower and authorize His followers to speak words that carried power. He had the audacity to tell believers to have faith in God—literally, have the faith of God—and speak to things.

Jesus showed us that real faith—the faith of God—is a two-part equation. Faith is made up of what we believe in our hearts and what we say with our mouths. The apostle Paul taught the same thing. He gave us the anatomy of faith when he said, "And since we have the same spirit of faith, according to what is written, 'I believed and therefore I spoke,' we also believe and therefore speak," (2 Cor. 4:13).

If we are going to live a supernatural, power-packed, dynamic, Jesus-filled life of faith that causes fig trees to dry up from the roots or that causes mountains to move, we are going to have to believe God and speak words.

If You Want Your Mountains to Move

Jesus told us what to do if we want to see a mountain move in our lives. He told us to speak directly to the mountain. Jesus said, "For assuredly, I say to you, whoever says to this mountain . . . " (Mark 11:22).

He didn't say talk to God *about* the mountain; He definitely instructed us to *talk to* the mountain. Interestingly, Jesus did not tell us to *pray about* the mountain; He said speak to it. He did NOT say, "For assuredly, I say to you, whoever *prays to God about* this mountain, 'Be removed and be cast into the sea,' and does not doubt in his heart, but believes that those things he *prays* will be done, he will have whatever he *prays*."

However, instead of talking directly to our mountains, we often pray to God about our mountains. We pray, "Oh God, I need help with this mountain. See how big my mountain is? I ask You to move that massive thing." (Prayer is a good thing, a godly thing, a great thing! But in this verse, Jesus didn't instruct us to pray about the mountain; He told us to speak to it. I'll save the equally important subject of words and prayer for another book.)

Jesus told us to speak to the mountain. Have you talked to a mountain—any obstacle, giant or challenge—lately? Go ahead. Be bold. Take Jesus at His Word. Have the faith of God and speak directly to your mountain.

We Must Believe What We Say

When we speak to our mountains, Jesus told us to believe what we say. Notice this little phrase, "whoever . . . believes that those things he says will be done, he will have whatever he says," (Mark 11:23). Jesus said in order for our words to have any mountain-moving power, we must believe what we say, and we must believe what we say will be done. That's a pretty amazing truth.

But this is where some of us mess things up. We say a lot of things we don't believe, and we train ourselves to not believe what we say. We make off-the-cuff remarks all the time—remarks we don't really believe—and when we need to say things we do believe, our hearts are confused. For example, we say things like, "Hey, let's get together for lunch." But, in reality we don't believe those words, and we have no intention of getting together for lunch. We say it because it sounds friendly.

We say, "I'll be praying for you," but in truth, we don't really believe those words—it is just the Christian thing to say. We know we will probably forget to pray for them, and in doing so, we've trained ourselves to say words we don't believe.

This is a problem! If we want mountains to move, Jesus told us we must believe the words we say to those mountains. If we are in the habit of speaking words we don't believe, then we will be conflicted when we actually need to believe what we say.

What's the solution? Get in the habit of only saying words you believe. Then, when you need to believe the words you speak to a mountain in front of you, your heart won't be confused. You will believe what you say.

Remember what Jesus said: "Whoever says to this mountain, 'Be removed and be cast into the sea,' and does not doubt in his heart, but believes that those things he says will be done, he will have whatever he says," (Mark 11:23). We must believe what we say.

When Life Is Hard

Before we go any further, let's talk about an interesting phenomenon that occurs regarding what we believe in our hearts and say with our mouths. Jesus told us to believe what we say. So sometimes we have to start off saying things by faith, even if at first we don't feel very strong in faith. In fact, we may be so discouraged we barely believe God's Word or what we are saying. We may only have a mustard-seed-sized belief. That's okay— that's all we need to get started. If we will get started in saying what the Word says, more faith will come.

If you're going through a season where life is hard, you don't feel God's presence in your life, you feel like a failure, nothing is going your way and you're just about ready to give up on everything; you are the perfect candidate for putting God's Word to work.

Be encouraged by this illustration. Let's say there is a tiny, sliver of mustard seed faith somewhere in the deep recesses of your heart. Somewhere from deep inside you do have a faded belief that with God all things may be possible. You have no idea how that could ever become a reality in your life, but for kicks, you decide to give this faith-filled words thing a try. By faith, you eke out a few words with a bit of mustard seed faith. You speak to your mountain, "Mountain of failure, gloom and doom—jump into the sea."

The mountain laughs at you. It mocks you. It tries to intimidate you. It doesn't budge. Your mustard seed bit of faith looks at the mountain and says, "Oh really?" You're faith still seems small, but you hold steady and you repeat your words to that mountain. "Mountain of failure, gloom and doom—jump into the sea!" and then you go about your life.

A few days later, a good Christian friend says to you, "Hey, cheer up! If God is for you, who can be against you?" You smile. You think he just quoted a verse from somewhere in the Bible. Later you discover it was Romans 8:31. Your mustard seed of faith starts to grow in your heart.

The next day you're visiting your mother-in-law, and you see an old plaque on her kitchen wall with this Scripture, "Now thanks be to God who always leads us in triumph in Christ, and through us diffuses the fragrance of His knowledge in every place," (2 Cor. 2:14). You make a mental note, and something clicks in your heart.

A few days later you see your Bible under a stack of magazines, and you decide to crack it open. It happens to fall open to Psalm 5:12:

"For You, O Lord, will bless the righteous; with favor You will surround him as with a shield."

All of these Scriptures start to go through your mind and heart. Your faith is growing. You think, *Maybe God is for me after all. Maybe Jesus will lead me in triumph and victory. Maybe God would surround me with favor.* You're still not feeling it, but you do believe the Bible is true, so, once again with a little more oomph, you speak to that big mountain of failure that's been staring you down.

"Listen here, Failure Mountain, God is for me, so who can be against me? He always leads me in triumph in Christ. The Lord surrounds me with favor." You say it three or four times. You decide to keep at it, and you say these words of faith another ten times.

Here's what will happen: faith will come.

The Bible says, "So then faith comes by hearing, and hearing by the word of God," (Rom. 10:17). So, even though at first you don't feel like God's Word is true for you, if you will continue to say what God says—a dozen or a hundred or a thousand more times—your ears will continue to hear it and your heart will start to believe it and faith will come! It won't take long, and your mustard-seed-sized faith will grow and turn into real mountain-moving faith. You will know because you know because you know that God is for you, so who can be against you? He always leads you in triumph in Christ. The Lord surrounds you with favor.

By the 3000th time you've said it, that mustard-seed-sized faith has grown into mountain-moving-sized faith, and you are ready to shout at that mountain of failure with gusto. The next thing you know you'll be saying, "You wanna a piece of me? Listen here, Failure Mountain, I've got some news for you. God is for me, so who can be against me? He always leads me in triumph in Christ. I am a winner. I always come out on top. I succeed, and He prospers the work of my hands. The Lord surrounds me with favor. Everywhere I go the Lord is with me, and He's opening doors left and right. I am filled with His favor, blessings and goodness. Failure Mountain, I command you to take a flying leap into the sea because, as I said, according to God's Word, 'God is for me, so who can be against me?'"

At this point, that mountain has no choice. According to Jesus, it has to jump into the sea because you have exercised your faith in God by speaking to that mountain and commanding it to be removed and cast out of your life. When we get to the place where our faith is based on God's Word and we do not doubt in our hearts but believe the things we say will come to pass, we will have what we say.

Get the idea? Is there a mountain standing between you and God's will for your life? Are you ready to tell it to take a flying leap? Do exactly what Jesus did; follow His instructions. Have faith in God. Speak to your mountain. Don't doubt in your heart. Believe the things you say will be done. In time, you will have what you say.

CHAPTER 6:

War of Words

Does the truth about the power of our words almost seem too simplistic or too good to be true? Surely, there has to be a catch, right? We must be overlooking or overemphasizing something. Is it possible that God really wants us to take Him at His Word? Did Jesus really mean what He said when He told us to talk to mountains? Is the power of life and death really in our words? Does the spiritual law of words really work?

Like physical laws, spiritual laws work in tandem with other laws. This subject, the law of words, doesn't work in isolation. While I am focusing on the subject of words in this book, I am not suggesting that anyone should minimize or detach from the application of other spiritual laws, wisdom, discernment, integrity, ethics, the fruit of the Spirit and common sense as that person appropriates this truth. The best thing to do as a growing follower of Christ is to seek a balanced, comprehensive understanding of any biblical topic, and avoid going into unhealthy ditches. Let's talk about a few extremes.

Whack Jobs and Critics

Anytime you talk about a powerful, biblical principle, there will be several extreme fringe camps: the totally sincere yet excessive, hyper-spiritual, over-the-top whack jobs; and the totally mean-spirited, cynical, rude, scornful, suspicious, doubtful, mocking critics. Welcome to the Christian life.

Concerning the Whack Jobs: These are genuine believers. They are usually good people that have just enough Bible knowledge to be dangerous to themselves. They get an *A* for effort but a *D* for wisdom in misunderstanding or misapplying the Word and the truth of speaking faith-filled words.

When people do weird, eccentric things in the name of "faith confession," it gives the whole topic a black eye; and the enemy uses these crazy things to turn people off from a real truth that the Lord intended for us to understand and apply.

Here are a few examples. We heard about one lady who spoke to her belly button and told it to leave her body. That's flaky. Another person thought he could confess his neighbor's car into his own driveway. These are extreme examples of unbalanced people trying to manipulate God's Word into being something it clearly is not. Just because there are a few out-of-balance extremists doesn't mean we should throw out the whole concept and truth of God's Word on this subject.

Concerning the Critics: We've all known well-meaning critics who couldn't reconcile the idea that God would give mankind the authority to speak words that carried the power of life and death. Because of their lack of understanding on this subject, they've taken joy in using hurtful comments to belittle believers who embrace God's law of words: "Are you one of those 'name it, claim it,' 'confess it, possess it' Christians? Do you really believe that you can talk to whatever mountain you want? Who do you think you are? You're trying to act like God."

There will always be naysayers. Just because a few cynics without any revelation knowledge of God's Word on this subject make harsh comments, it doesn't mean they are right in their understanding or that they are authorities on the subject.

God's Word is the authority. We need to let the Word give us the balance and answers we need. Let's dive in a little deeper.

Words We Live By

The Lord has authorized and deputized us to speak faith-filled words. That is clear and well documented from Scripture. But here's the important question: we are authorized to speak words based on what? Based on our whims? Based on carnal desires? Can we "confess and

The foundation for speaking faith-filled words is God's Word.

possess" or "name and claim" anything we want? Absolutely not. The foundation for speaking faith-filled words is God's Word.

Jesus made it clear, "It is written, 'Man shall not live by bread alone, but by every word that proceeds from the mouth of God,'" (Matt. 4:4). In this response to the temptation He faced, Jesus revealed a huge secret for living a faith-filled, destiny-laden, blessed and favored life. We must live by God's words. We can and should have absolute confidence in confessing, possessing, naming and claiming the things God has spoken to us from His Word.

The word *word* in Matthew 4:4 is the Greek word: *rhema*. Rhema means "that which is or has been uttered by the living voice, thing spoken, word." We often simplify that by understanding rhema as God's spoken word or the living word; something that is spoken to us by His Spirit in the now.

In other words, Jesus is telling us that man does not live by food alone but by the rhema word that comes from God's mouth. We are to live by every rhema word—spoken or living—that comes from God's mouth to our hearts. What does this look like? Has the Lord ever spoken or quickened a Scripture to your heart? In other words, as you were pondering things, waiting on God, praying, reading the Bible or listening to the Word or a sermon, has the Lord *spoken* it to you? Did a particular Scripture or truth speak to your heart in the now or present tense? If so, that was a rhema word.

Perhaps you've said, "That verse spoke to me" or "God's Word lit up in my heart" or "it seemed like that Scripture jumped off the page." It doesn't necessarily mean you felt goose bumps or heard an angelic choir, but it does mean that God's living Word was quickened in your spirit. When the Word is quickened to your heart, that's a rhema word. A rhema word is a now word, a living word, one that comes from the mouth of God. Jesus said these are the type of words we are to live by, and these are the words we are to speak.

Led by the Word

When I look back over my life, it is chronicled as much by the Word of God—specifically the living words God has spoken to my heart—as by the years on the calendar. Whenever I needed God's direction, I sought answers in His Word. Thankfully, His Word is a lamp for our feet and once I received a word from God, it was my job to believe, act upon and speak those words. The Lord has been faithful and I've experienced the joy of His supernatural guidance. Here are a couple of examples from my early Christian life to encourage you to consider the words the Lord is speaking to you.

It was 1982—Luke 2:39: A year after I graduated from Boston University, I felt prompted of the Lord to move to California to help a friend who was going through a rough time. I didn't know how long I would be there, but I knew I was on an assignment to do what I could to help this young lady put her feet on the path the Lord had for her. Within a few weeks of my arrival, it was apparent she was not interested in my help or input. I talked to her as much as she would allow, but it was evident her heart was not open to the things I felt the Lord had sent me to deliver.

On top of her lack of receptivity, I was not enjoying California. (I know that's hard to believe, but I really didn't like California under the circumstances.) So after a month or so, I prayed, "Lord, what's the deal? This person doesn't seem very receptive. I am planting all the seeds I know how to plant, now what? Do you want me to stay in California, or should I move back to Michigan?"

At that point in my Christian life, I had learned it's better to be in God's will than to do my own thing. I knew I needed to hear from God. I couldn't just do what I wanted to do; I couldn't go on my whim—I needed to live by His word. So, I got into the Word to see what the Lord had to say to me.

One day I was reading in Luke, and I came across this verse, "When Joseph and Mary had done everything required by the Law of the Lord, they returned to Galilee to their own town of Nazareth," (Luke 2:39 NIV). As soon as I read those words, the Lord spoke to my heart; and I said, "Hallelujah!" I felt I had done everything the Lord asked of me in sharing His Word with this individual, and this Scripture was the confirmation I needed to return to my own town in Michigan. At that point I could speak with faith-filled confidence, "I am moving back home—in the will of God!" That's exactly what I did. The Lord worked it all out, and I returned home.

Years later, all the seeds sown on that trip and in other conversations with my friend eventually produced great fruit. Today, this person is serving the Lord in ministry and reaching many people for Him.

It was 1983—Psalm 37:3: I was twenty-four years old and felt confident the Lord had called me to the ministry. At the time, I was working for an orthopedic surgeon and assisting him as he wrote medical textbooks. I was also seeking the Lord about going to Bible school.

In July 1983, as I eagerly looked into my options for obtaining more ministry training, the surgeon I worked for came into my office and asked me, "Would you stay on and work for me one more year?"

I was not excited about that offer. In my heart, I wanted to go to Bible school. In my flesh, I didn't want to continue working in the medical field. So, I got into the Word to hear from God. I knew I needed to live by His words.

One day as I was reading in Psalms, I came across Psalm 37:3, "Trust in the Lord and do good; dwell in the land and cultivate faithfulness," (NASB).

This verse of Scripture leapt off the page and settled in my heart—but I didn't want it to. I didn't like what I had read. Have you ever tried to erase a verse from the Bible? I didn't want to "dwell in the land and cultivate faithfulness"; I wanted to go to Bible school.

As I listened to the Lord, I felt the Holy Spirit speaking to me, "It's not the right time. For now, I need you to dwell in this land and cultivate faithfulness." I was bummed, but I obeyed. I realized God was serious and He wanted me to cultivate faithfulness.

I wanted to pass this test the first time around, so I decided to get my words working in the right direction. Instead of complaining, moaning and groaning about my job or about living in Michigan, I decided when people asked me what I was doing, I'd say, "The Lord told me to dwell in the land and cultivate faithfulness, and that's what I am going to do."

It was 1984—Deuteronomy 1:6-8: During that year, I continued working for the orthopedic surgeon while cultivating faithfulness. I also experimented with some creative ideas, and in my spare time I designed several Christian greeting cards. A few bookstores started carrying them, and somehow my cards reached the desk of the president of a large Christian gift products company in Minnesota.

One day, out of the blue, I received a phone call from the president's assistant inviting me to come to Minneapolis to talk to them about a position they wanted to create for me. I flew to Minneapolis, stayed with the president and his wife, and enjoyed the chance to get to know them. I also toured the facility and learned firsthand the heartbeat of their company.

War of Words

The position they offered to create for me was creative director. It would be my job to create, design and develop all kinds of Christian products from bookmarks to plaques to calendars to greeting cards. The sky would be the limit. As a creative person with a degree in communications, this was what I would have called my dream job. If I could have written a perfect job description for me, this would have been it. On top of that, I had quickly come to admire the company president and his wife and would have been honored to work for them.

I knew I needed to pray. I needed to hear from God. I still desired to go to Bible school but this job offer was almost too good to be true. What did the Lord want me to do? I needed a word from God to live by. I wanted to follow the plan God had already blessed, rather than asking God to bless the plan I desired to follow.

I spent some extra time praying, seeking the Lord and getting into the Bible. Thankfully, the Lord spoke to my heart through several passages of Scripture. His word confirmed the desire He had put in my heart to attend Bible school. One particular passage stood out. As I read my Bible, I came upon these verses:

The Lord our God spoke to us in Horeb, saying: "You have dwelt long enough at this mountain. Turn and take your journey, and go to the mountains of the Amorites, to all the neighboring places in the plain, in the mountains and in the lowland, in the South and on the seacoast, to the land of the Canaanites and to Lebanon, as far as the great river, the River Euphrates. See, I have set the land before you; go in and possess the land."

Deuteronomy 1:6-8

That settled it. God knew I had dwelt at my current mountain long enough, and through His Word He gave me direction; it was time to turn and take my journey. I contacted the company president to thank him for his consideration and to decline the job offer. Then, I started packing my bags for Bible school!

Since I had God's word on it, I had complete confidence that I was smack dab in the center of God's will as I turned down the job of my dreams and headed off to Bible school. It was easy to get my words in agreement with His; by faith I could declare, confess, possess, name, claim and speak to any mountain that got in my way. I knew I could trust the Lord to completely order my steps and meet all of my needs as I prepared for ministry, and He did.

How about you? What decisions are you facing? What direction do you need? Which words does God want you to live by? If you need the Lord's guidance for any area of your life, spend some extra time in fellowship with the Lord and His Word, and He will speak a word to your heart. When He does, you will have great confidence to believe it, speak it and live it.

CHAPTER 7

Frame Your World

Have you ever built a house or been involved with a construction project? If so, you know how important the foundation and frame is. Once the foundation is poured, it's critical that the framing—the beams, posts and studs—goes up plumb. A skewed frame will mess up the whole building. How would drywall look on a wall that wasn't built at a 90-degree angle to the floor? What would curtains look like on windows hung on a wall framed at 45 degrees? Can you imagine how funky a house or building would look with pieces of the framework sticking out from a wall or ceiling in random places? A building without a strong foundation and a proper, balanced, well-built frame will be a structural disaster.

In the Beginning

God is the Master Builder, and He built the whole universe with words. He laid the foundation and framed our world with His words. He made the visible world from things that were not visible: "By faith we understand that the worlds were framed by the word of God, so that the things which are seen were not made of things which are visible," (Heb. 11:3).

Here's how it happened: "In the beginning God created the heavens and the earth. . . . Then God said, 'Let there be light'; and there was light," (Gen. 1:1,3). God's words created substance. The Lord spoke words; the Holy Spirit took those words and formed protons, neutrons and electrons, which formed atoms; those atoms made matter; that matter became everything in our material, physical world. Everything in all of creation was created with words.

God, through His Son Jesus, continues to uphold the world with His Word:

> He is the sole expression of the glory of God [the Light-being, the out-raying or radiance of the divine], and He is the perfect imprint and very image of [God's] nature, upholding and maintaining and guiding and propelling the universe by His mighty word of power.
>
> Hebrews 1:3 AMP

God spoke invisible words, and the visible world was. God's words brought things that are not visible into the visible realm. This is God's principle of faith in operation: "God, who gives life to the dead and calls those things which do not exist as though they did," (Rom. 4:17).

Words Frame Our World

In the same way, God frames, upholds, maintains, guides and propels the visible world with His invisible words. Our visible, personal world can and should be framed by God's invisible Word. As we put His Word in our hearts and mouths, calling "things which do not exist as though they did," (Rom. 4:17), we will see Him frame our world and do amazing things, "so that the things which are seen were not made of things which are visible," (Heb. 11:3).

We can frame our world—our walk with the Lord, our emotional and mental health, our physical health and strength, our relationships, marriage, family, ministries, finances and our success in life—by speaking God's Word.

How's your world being framed? Are you building your life upon the strong, godly foundation of a personal relationship with Jesus Christ? Is your life plumb and congruent with God's best? Are things coming together for you? Are windows and doors opening for you? If you want to live the supernatural, victorious Christian life, you'll have to get your mouth in agreement with God's Word. Over time, those words will frame your world. Are you ready to say the kinds of words that will frame your life the way God intends? Are you ready to call things that do not exist as though they did?

Today, frame your world by saying what God says.

Faith or Denial?

When it comes to framing our world with words, there's a fine but clearly defined line between faith and denial. Let's look at the difference between "calling things that *are not* as though they *are*" versus "calling things that *are* as though they *are not.*"

Sometimes, in our zeal, we hear a little bit of teaching on this subject and without a strong, balanced understanding of God's Word and the principles of faith and confession, we run off and misapply the Word. The Bible never tells us to deny the reality of our world and speak as if certain things don't exist. Instead, by faith, we are called to change the realities in our world, by "calling things that are not, as though they were," (Rom. 4:17 NIV). God wants us to speak in the "as-though" tense. Let's look at it.

If we are tired or weak, we shouldn't say, "I'm not weak. I'm not weak. I'm not weak." That's just a denial of reality. We should supersede reality with the truth. We should call things as though they were and say, "The Bible says, 'Let the weak say "I am strong,"' (Joel 3:10). So, today, I call myself strong. I am strong in the Lord and the power of His might."

If we are sick, we shouldn't say: "I don't believe I am sick." "I'm not sick." "I don't have a broken bone." "I don't have cancer." "I don't have back pain." "I call myself not sick." Again, that's denial, and God never tells us to go into denial. We can't call things that are as though they are not, but we can call things that are not as though they are.

If we are sick, we can trump the reality of that sickness with the truth and power of God's Word. If we are facing an illness or disease, we should call things that are not as though they were by saying what God's Word says, "In Jesus' name, I call things that are not as though they were. So, I call my immune system strong. I call my body healed, healthy and whole. I agree with God's Word, and His wisdom and healing power is at work in my body. I call my bones strong. I call my body free from cancer. I call my body free from back pain. He carried my sickness and pains; by Jesus stripes, my body is healed. He is the God that heals me. Jesus is my Healer and Great Physician, and He leads me down the best pathway for my health and healing. I believe God's wisdom is mine, and His healing power is at work in my body. He heals me of all my diseases."

There is a difference between truth and reality. Our experiences and circumstances may be our reality at a given point in time, but God's Word is truth. Truth always trumps reality. We should not deny reality, but we can and should trump it with truth. Can you see the distinction?

By agreeing with God's Word, we can call things that are not as though they were, and this opens the door for God's power, wisdom and divine intervention to frame our world with complete wholeness. As it relates to healing and wholeness, He may heal us supernaturally, or He may lead us down a variety of pathways for restoration. The Lord may instruct us to change our diet or eating patterns; He may lead us to get more rest or exercise; He may direct our steps to a specialist; or all of the above. Our job is to get the law of words working in the right direction so God's truth frames our world.

God never tells us to deny reality; He just instructs us to supersede reality with Truth.

God never tells us to deny reality; He just instructs us to supersede reality with Truth. Don't call things that are as though they're not. But do call things that are not as though they are. Frame your world with the Word.

The "As-Though" Tense

As soon as I began to understand these things, I began to call things that were not as though they were. I started to frame my world with words. I was single and living in an apartment, and I started saying, "Someday I'm going to have a four-bedroom house with a pool or one that is on a lake. I don't really care. Either option is fine. I just want to live near water. Someday, I'm going to have a four-bedroom house with a pool or one that is on a lake."

When Jeff and I got married, our first home while we lived in Tulsa and attended Bible school was a small townhouse. It didn't have four bedrooms or a lake, but there was a community pool. Then we moved into a rented two-bedroom house. Again, no pool and no lake. I continued to say, "Someday I'm going to have a four-bedroom house with a pool or one that is on a lake. I don't really care. Either option is fine. I just want to live near water."

When we moved back to Michigan to start a church, we spent most of our money on the start-up costs associated with the church plant. In that season, we lived on a shoestring budget, and the only thing we could afford to purchase was a little 800-square-foot cottage. This cottage was microscopic. My husband is 6' 6", and I am 5' 10", so we are not small people, but we lived in a puny house. This was not the four-bedroom house with a pool or one that was on the lake, but it was near a lake, so at least we were still making progress.

I continued to call things that were not as though they were. Although it was a very difficult season of delayed gratification, I continued to frame my world with words: "Someday we're going to live in a four-bedroom house with a pool or one that is on a lake."

Then it happened. The church was firmly planted and growing, and the Lord led us to the perfect house. We moved into a four-bedroom house with a pool. We were thrilled. A few years later, as the kids grew, we moved into another house—this time a five-bedroom house with a pool. Bonus! It didn't happen overnight, but eventually the invisible became visible.

What about you? What are you saying about your home? Your marriage? Your kids? Your life? Get started calling things that are not as though they were. Frame your world.

Copycats

Let's address a question that usually comes up when we talk about framing our world with words. Sometimes people struggle with the idea that they can and should speak faith-filled words because they wonder if they are being presumptuous in taking God at His Word and employing the law of words. *After all*, they think, *who am I to call things that are not as though they were? I'm not God.*

It's true; we are not God, but God Himself told us we are to imitate Him: "Be imitators of God, therefore, as dearly loved children," (Eph. 5:1 NIV). Listen to the *Amplified* version of this same verse, "Therefore be imitators of God [copy Him and follow His example], as well-beloved children [imitate their father]."

Have you ever seen a young child copy his mom or dad? Kids always mimic their parents, yet we never rebuke them for doing so, do we? In fact, when kids imitate their parents' good behavior, their character, their integrity or their method of operation, we commend them. How much more should we imitate our heavenly Father? He is a faith God who speaks faith words in the "as-though" tense—we should too.

Jesus Will Build His Church

We've seen the law of words work throughout the years of our ministry.

In 1991, we pioneered Kalamazoo Valley Family Church (now Valley Family Church), in Kalamazoo, Michigan, with a team of five adults and four kids. With a big vision, we made plans to launch the church with our whopping nine people. At the time, I was pregnant, and the other woman was pregnant; so we knew the church would definitely grow in nine months. We were counting on a church growth population boom of two, but in order to fulfill the vision God had given us, we knew we needed to exercise our faith and put the law of words to work.

We were aware of the very low statistics on successful church plants; we knew the average-size church in America was around 150 people; and we heard about the toll ministry can take on marriages and family. We also knew the burning passion and vision God put in our hearts for reaching people with the good news of the gospel of Jesus Christ and the power of His Word.

Immediately, we started to frame our church world with words. We adopted this motto, "Kalamazoo Valley Family Church reaching southwest Michigan." That's right; all nine of us were going to make a big impact on southwest Michigan. (We laughed and cried over that motto; it was definitely faith speaking.)

After we officially launched the church with our grand opening service, a core group of about forty people remained. We weren't exactly reaching southwest Michigan but at least moving in the right direction. After a year or so, we had grown to 125; and then we had a big push to break the 200-barrier, and we did. Then we grew to 250, then 300, then 400 and then 500 people. Slowly but surely the things which were becoming visible were being made from the things which were not visible.

By 1999, we were thankful that 500 people attended church each weekend. We still weren't "reaching southwest Michigan" or even making a big dent in the region, but we continued to work hard, living by faith, teaching the Word, preaching the gospel, ministering to people and framing our world with words.

Year after year we saw the invisible turn into the visible. By following the Lord, believing His Word, being led by the Spirit, embracing the principles of faith and employing the law of words, we were laborers together with God as we watched Jesus build His church. The church grew to 600, then 800, then 1000, then 1400, then 2000 and it continued. We changed our name to Valley Family Church, and these days 4000 people attend VFC each weekend. We're getting closer and closer to seeing those faith-filled words: "reaching southwest Michigan" come to pass.

How about you? Are you framing your world, your family, your business or your ministry with words? Are you speaking the language of faith in the "as-though" tense? Stay with it knowing your faith-filled words are giving substance to the things hoped for: "Now faith is the substance of things hoped for, the evidence of things not seen. . . . By faith we understand that the worlds were framed by the word of God, so that the things which are seen were not made of things which are visible," (Heb. 11:1,3).

CHAPTER 8:

I Called It

The "I called it" rule. No doubt, you or your kids have employed this rule. It seems to be a universal code among kids—one they intuitively know from birth.

The "I called it" rule goes like this: it's early Saturday morning, and the kids are getting ready for a soccer game, basketball league or volleyball tournament. Just before everyone walks out the door to pile in the car, one of the kids shouts out, "I call shotgun!" (In kid-speak, *shotgun* means the front seat of the car.)

What does "I call it" mean? If you call it, it's yours. By calling it, you get the right to sit in the front seat. All of the other kids understand this rule, and they comply. (They may not like it, but if someone calls it, everyone still complies.) Children are letter of the law on the "I called it" rule. If Tommy calls shotgun, he gets shotgun; and there is no argument about it. It doesn't matter whose turn it is or who gets to the front seat first; what matters is who called it. All kids understand that by calling it, they have established their rights with the law of words.

We've seen this law in operation in our family many times. I distinctly remember one episode where I had to enforce the "I called it" rule. One day as we were leaving the house, our youngest son, Eric, shouted, "I call shotgun." When the entire family started to pile in the car, Annie, our second oldest daughter, wanted to sit shotgun, but it didn't take long for the other kids to set Annie straight by telling her Eric called it already. She looked at me for sympathy and a reversal. I said, "I don't know what to tell you, Annie. Eric called it." Everyone understood.

Wired Into Our DNA?

How do kids intuitively pick up on the universal "I called it" rule? Have you noticed that kids use this rule for everything—which child gets to push the elevator buttons in hotels, do chores around the house, eat leftovers, play video games—you name it.

A few years ago, my husband Jeff and I were out of town, so we asked our oldest daughter, Meghan, who was nineteen years old and in college, to come home to watch the kids for us. She took the "I called it" rule to another level.

When we called home to check on the kids, I asked Meghan how it was going. She said, "It's going fine, but I had one problem."

I asked, "What's the problem?"

She said, "I had to ground Luke." (Luke, her younger brother, was fourteen years old at the time.) I was surprised and not even sure a sister could ground a brother, so I covered up the phone to talk to Jeff.

"Meghan grounded Luke. Can she do that? Can a sister ground a brother?" I was thinking, *Luke's a big kid; he could beat her up if he wanted too. Does he know that?*

Jeff reminded me, "Meghan's in charge. If she called it, then so it is. If she grounded Luke, Luke is grounded."

Luke complied with Meghan's grounding because she established it with words, and they both knew when we got home, we would support and back up Meghan's decision.

The same thing is true when we "call it" according to God's Word. The same God who has authorized us to speak faith-filled words backs us up. We've been made in God's image; perhaps the I-called-it reflex is hardwired into our DNA. There seems to be a God-given instinct in all of us to "call" things. I suppose we should not be surprised; after all, God was the originator and first One to put the "I called it" rule to work when He called all of creation into existence: "God, who gives life to the dead and calls those things which do not exist as though they did," (Rom. 4:17).

Adam: The First Human to Call It

After creation, God made man and authorized him to speak. Adam was the first human being to ever speak words. God launched the law of words with Adam. He gave Adam the authority to use his voice to establish things:

> Out of the ground the Lord God formed every beast of the field and every bird of the air, and brought them to Adam to see what he would call them. And whatever Adam called each living creature, that was its name. So Adam gave names to all cattle, to the birds of the air, and to every beast of the field.
>
> Genesis 2:19,20

Can you imagine the joy the Lord must have experienced when He watched His man employ the law of words to call things? Whatever Adam called each living creature, that was its name. The power of life and death was in Adam's tongue.

Why did God want Adam to name the animals? The Lord could have given each animal a proper name Himself. God had the wisdom and ability to name the animals, but He chose to give that power and authority to Adam. He enabled Adam to call it—to establish something with words. We might say that Adam was the first person who said, "I called it." He called it, and so it was.

In studying the Word, it seems God still wants His men and women to call things. Are you employing the law of words in your life? Are you calling things in accordance with God's Word? Are you using your voice to call it? What do you call your life? What do you call your business? What do you call your body? What do you call your mind? What do you call your marriage? What do you call your kids?

My husband, Jeff, tells a story about his experience calling things when he was in business. He was a young Christian in the commercial and industrial lighting sales business, and his customers were wholesalers and distributors who carried his products on their shelves.

When Jeff began to learn about the power of faith-filled words, he decided to put God's Word to work. This was in Michigan in the eighties during one of Michigan's worst recessions. Whenever Jeff would visit his customers, he would see all of his products on their shelves. He made a point to walk by his products, and as he did, he would point to them and say, "I call you sold in Jesus' name." At first, some of his wholesaler's thought he was crazy. However, it didn't take long for his customers to see that Jeff was onto something. You can guess what happened. His products started selling while his competitors' products sat on the shelves. The "I called it" rule worked.

Moses: He Wouldn't Talk to a Rock

Moses was a great man of God. He was mightily used of the Lord as a prophet and deliverer. He was also very humble and known as the meekest man on earth. But, Moses made one big mistake that cost him greatly. Moses wasn't willing to call it. Moses' disobedience in the area of words cost him. This is a lesson we all need to heed. Let's look at the story.

The Lord said to Moses, "Take the staff, and you and your brother Aaron gather the assembly together. Speak to that rock before their eyes and it will pour out its water. You will bring water out of the rock for the community so they and their livestock can drink."

So Moses took the staff from the Lord's presence, just as he commanded him. He and Aaron gathered the assembly together in front of the rock and Moses said to them, "Listen, you rebels, must we bring you water out of this rock?" Then Moses raised his arm and struck the rock twice with his staff. Water gushed out, and the community and their livestock drank.

But the Lord said to Moses and Aaron, "Because you did not trust in me enough to honor me as holy in the sight of the Israelites, you will not bring this community into the land I give them."

Numbers 20:7-12 NIV

What did the Lord ask Moses to do? What caused God to become so angry with Moses to the point that Moses disqualified himself from entering the Promised Land? It was about words.

The Lord told Moses to gather the congregation and speak to the rock before their eyes. God promised when Moses did this, water would spring forth from the rock and give drink to the congregation and their animals. Moses thought he had a better idea. He decided to strike the rock twice with his rod, instead of speaking to the rock.

Moses did what a lot of us do: he began to reason, and he allowed his reason, logic, feelings and flesh to dominate his thinking and his behavior. Perhaps he was angry with the children of Israel, and he thought, *What good is speaking to a rock? These people are dying of thirst, and I need to do something dramatic. I'll just beat the water out of these rocks!* The most amazing thing is although Moses was disobedient to the Lord's command, water did gush forth from the rock. In His mercy, the Lord caused water to supernaturally spring forth to quench the thirst of the congregation and their animals, but Moses' disobedience cost him. The Lord did not allow Moses to enter the Promised Land; he was only able to see if from afar. His disobedience in not speaking words cost him the promise of God.

There is no doubt the Lord loved Moses. The Bible is full of stories about Moses and his faith, humility and love for the Lord; but it was his disobedience and the lack of words that caused Moses' problem. The Lord loves us too. Has your apathy, passivity or disobedience in speaking faith-filled words cost you your Promised Land at times?

Silence Is Not Always Golden

Martin Luther King, Jr., once said, "Our lives begin to end the day we become silent about things that matter." Silence is not always golden.

If the enemy can't get us to disobey God's command to speak words, he may go the opposite direction and deceive us into silence. We need to remember if the devil can't get us to speak words of death, doubt, unbelief and negativity; he'll do his best to silence us into not speaking any words at all.

> We need to remember if the devil can't get us to speak words of death, doubt, unbelief and negativity; he'll do his best to silence us into not speaking any words.

Plan A—The devil wants us to speak words of death.

Plan B—The devil wants us to be silent.

The devil certainly doesn't want us to "call it" or say anything that carries the power of life. So, if he can't get us to cooperate with Plan A by speaking words of death, destruction and evil; he'd rather have us silent under Plan B. He'd rather do all the talking. He'd rather yap in our ears all day with lies, deceptions and untruths about God, His Word and His promises. He'd rather talk us into discouragement and depression and keep us locked up in a silent prison.

For example, the Bible says, "Let the redeemed of the Lord say so," (Ps. 107:2). We need to obey God's Word and say so. If we are redeemed, the Lord wants us to say it. We need to say things like, "I am redeemed. I am redeemed from sin and death to eternal life. I am redeemed from sickness and disease to health and wholeness. I am redeemed from poverty and lack to abundance and more than enough. I am the redeemed, and I say so."

Of course, the enemy would rather have us NOT say so. He'd rather keep us bound by silence so we do not experience the benefits of our redemption. We can count on it—if he can't get us to speak negative things; he'd rather keep us locked up in silence and the prison of sin, death, sickness, disease, poverty, lack and despair.

What has the Lord told you to say? Does He want you to "call it" in some areas? Has He told you to speak to a rock or your circumstances in order to enter your Promised Land? Don't be silent. Instead, make a decision to agree with God and get your mouth moving.

Name It and Claim It: God's Will

What about the idea of naming and claiming things? Can we "call it" when it comes to things like a spouse? A car? A job? A home?

No doubt God is looking for people who will put His Word in their hearts and mouths and lay claim to it. However, our ability to speak faith-filled words, to "call it," "name it and claim it" or "confess it and possess it" is absolutely contingent on those words being congruent with God's Word. As I have mentioned many times, God's Word is our foundation—I will never tire of saying that.

Our ability to speak faith-filled words, to "call it," "name it and claim it" or "confess it and possess it" is absolutely contingent on those words being congruent with God's Word.

89

Sometimes, people get zealous about a topic like this, and they decide they are going to start calling, claiming and confessing all kinds of things that may not even be scriptural. You can't just arbitrarily claim things. You have to be led by the Spirit and have a scriptural foundation or precedent in order to call, confess and possess or name and claim anything from God. Faith comes from hearing and hearing from God's Word. (Rom. 10:17.) Our foundation always has to be God's Word. Let's look at a few examples:

Can I Claim a Baby Boy or Baby Girl? Over the years we've talked to married couples who desired to have a baby. They've wondered if they could be specific and claim a baby boy or a baby girl. The answer to that question is answered with a question: which Scripture or verse would they stand on to claim the sex of a baby? It turns out there aren't any verses of Scripture to support the claiming of a boy or a girl. There are plenty of Scriptures that a couple could stand on concerning God's promise of children, a fruitful womb and a quiver full of children. By faith, a couple could claim children but not the specific gender of their baby.

We do see examples in the Word where the Lord told the parents in advance what gender their child would be. For example, Zechariah and Elizabeth were told they'd have a son, John. Joseph and Mary were told ahead of time they'd have a son, Jesus. Because of the foreknowledge information they received, they could say with confidence they were going to have a boy. Unless He specifically tells you the gender of your baby, you don't have scriptural grounds to claim the sex of a child. (What if Mary the mother of Jesus had claimed a girl?) We must trust the Lord in this area and leave the gender of our babies in His hands.

Can I Claim a Spouse? Here's another example. When my husband and I first began our ministry, we taught a large group of singles. The single people usually have one thing on their minds—finding a mate. Sometimes when we talked with those singles, they wondered how to pray and use their faith to find their dream wife or husband. Was it possible to confess and possess anyone they wanted to be their spouse? Uh . . . no!

Let's think about it. What if Mildred sees young Vern across the room? Can she say, "Ooooh, I think he's cute. I confess and possess Vern to be my husband."

Is that biblical? Of course not. Mildred can't claim Vern for her husband for many reasons. One major reason is because Vern has a will too. What if Vern doesn't want to be with Mildred? Vern has something to say about it. Besides that, which Scriptures does Mildred have for basing her claim on Vern? None.

What can Mildred believe for? If being married is the desire of her heart, she does have scriptural support to claim and ask God for a godly man—one with whom she is compatible, attracted to and with whom she could serve the Lord, have a family and fulfill God's will. That may or may not be Vern. Mildred could certainly pray for Vern, and she could ask the Lord about Vern. She could even strike up a friendship with Vern, but she couldn't claim him for a husband because there isn't any scriptural backing for it.

It's the same way with Biff. Let's say Biff is a 6 on the Hot-O-Meter, but he sees Bambi at the pool, and she's a 10. So, Biff says, "I claim Bambi. I confess that I will possess her to be my wife." Is that scriptural? Absolutely not. Biff can't claim Bambi because she has a will and a choice in the matter, particularly if she's a ten. She's probably not going to be interested in Mr. 6. There is no scriptural foundation for this type of thing.

Our foundation must always be the Word of God.

Call It According to the Word

Jesus said, "If you abide in me, and my words abide in you, you will ask what you desire and it shall be done for you," (John 15:7). It's interesting to note when Jesus used the word *ask*, it is translated as, "ask, desire, beg, call for, crave and require" in other places in the Bible. In Acts 16:29, this word is translated "called for."

Using this meaning, it would read like this, "If you abide in me, and my words abide in you, you will call for what you desire, and it shall be done for you."

Our foundation for asking or calling for things is based upon our abiding in Jesus and His Word, walking with God, relating to the Lord, having fellowship with God, being in His Word and letting Him talk to us. If we are abiding in Him and His Word, our desires will be His desires. Can you see that? Then, based on that foundation, we can ask, speak, call, claim and confess what we desire.

CHAPTER 9

A Grand Performance

Did you know the Lord's eyes are running to and fro all over the whole earth? They are. His eyes are running to and fro over the whole earth so He can show Himself strong on the behalf of those whose hearts are fully committed to Him. He's watching all the activity on earth looking for people and places where He can show up and put on a grand performance. It's true. "For the eyes of the Lord search back and forth across the whole earth, looking for people whose hearts are perfect toward him, so that he can show his great power in helping them," (2 Chron. 16:9 TLB).

Jeremiah

What are His eyes looking for? He's looking for those who believe Him and those who speak His Word. That's what He told Jeremiah. Jeremiah was called to be a prophet, a spokesperson for God, and he needed encouragement to

Get a Grip on Your Lip

be bold and confident in speaking God's Word. The Lord wanted to show Himself strong on Jeremiah's behalf. Let's look at what God said to Jeremiah:

> Then the word of the Lord came to me, saying: "Before I formed you in the womb I knew you; before you were born I sanctified you; I ordained you a prophet to the nations." Then said I: "Ah, Lord God! Behold, I cannot speak, for I am a youth." But the Lord said to me: "Do not say, 'I am a youth,' for you shall go to all to whom I send you, and whatever I command you, you shall speak. Do not be afraid of their faces, for I am with you to deliver you," says the Lord. Then the Lord put forth His hand and touched my mouth, and the Lord said to me: "Behold, I have put My words in your mouth. See, I have this day set you over the nations and over the kingdoms, to root out and to pull down, to destroy and to throw down, to build and to plant." Moreover the word of the Lord came to me, saying, "Jeremiah, what do you see?" And I said, "I see a branch of an almond tree." Then the Lord said to me, "You have seen well, for I am ready to perform My word."
>
> Jeremiah 1:4-12

Notice that last sentence, "Then the Lord said to me, 'You have seen well, for I am ready to perform My word.'" The *Amplified Bible* puts it this way, "Then said the Lord to me, 'You have seen well, for I am alert and active, watching over My word to perform it.'" The *New American*

Standard Bible says this, "I am watching over My word to perform it."

God has exalted His Word above His name, and He's always watching over His Word. (Ps. 138:2.) God wants to perform His Word in our lives, but in order to do so He needs His Word to be in our mouths. We need to give voice to God's Word on earth so He can perform it. Notice two things from this passage:

God wants to perform His Word in our lives, but in order to do so He needs His Word to be in our mouths.

First: Before God could use Jeremiah, He had to touch his mouth. God had a plan to use Jeremiah as a powerful prophet, and in order to do so, Jeremiah's mouth would have to be surrendered to the Lord and touched by God. The same is true today. If we want to live a power-packed life and be used of the Lord in a significant way, we will have to allow the Lord to touch our mouths.

Jeremiah started to head down the wrong road with his words, and God corrected him. Maybe Jeremiah was trying to be humble when he said, "I cannot speak, for I am a youth," or perhaps he was afraid or intimidated. In any event, God didn't appreciate it and immediately said, "Do not say, 'I am a youth.'" Then the Lord put forth his hand and touched Jeremiah's mouth.

That's how important it was. God had to touch Jeremiah's mouth to make sure he put his words to work in the right way. God didn't want Jeremiah to develop faith in his inability. God didn't want Jeremiah to be dominated by fear or intimidation or a false sense of humility. God needed Jeremiah to be strong in the Lord. He was able to help Jeremiah be strong by touching his mouth.

The same thing is true in our lives. God needs us to be strong in the Lord and confident in Him and His calling in our lives. We can be what God calls us to be. We can do what God calls us to do. We can have what God wants us to have. We need to develop faith in our ability through Christ, and we need to say what God says about these things.

In other words, if God has called you to speak; don't say you can't speak. You will develop faith in your inability. Don't say, "I'm just a child" or "I could never do that" or "I'm too old" or "I'm the wrong this" or "I'm the wrong that." Don't say it because you'll end up developing faith in your inabilities instead of God's ability in you. If God has called you to do something in your destiny and purpose, then you're going to need confidence to do it. Your confidence is going to need to be in the Lord. You are going to need internal strength to do it. Allow the Lord to touch your mouth, and make sure your words are working for you.

In this life, you're going to have enough opposition, so don't shoot yourself in your own foot with your words.

Whatever God has called you to do, you can do it. Don't be afraid;

don't put on a false air of humility; just agree with God. Perhaps you're called to business and to accumulating wealth to help finance the gospel. Maybe God has called you to the mission field. Perhaps God has called you to start a church. Maybe the Lord wants you to be a stay-at-home mom or adopt orphans from overseas. You can do everything He's called you to do. Agree with Him, and say what He says. In this life, you're going to have enough opposition, so don't shoot yourself in your own foot with your words.

Second: God wants to put on a big performance of His Word in our lives. In order to perform His Word, the Lord needs to find people who are in agreement with His Word and willing to speak it consistently. He needs people who will take Him at His Word.

The Bible tells us God is alert, active and watching over His Word to perform it. He's not asleep. He's not passive. He's paying attention. God is able and willing to put on a performance—He's able to perform His Word—when He finds His people speaking words of life in agreement with His Word.

At Creation, in the same way the Holy Spirit hovered over the face of the deep waiting to perform God's Word, the Lord is watching for His Word today. When God said, "Let there be light," the Spirit immediately performed those words and light was! When we give voice to God's Words in our lives, the Lord watches over that Word and performs it.

Think of it this way. The manifestation of God's Word in our lives is voice activated. That is, in order for God to perform the inherent potential of His Word in our lives, we need to activate it with our voice of faith.

It's a bit like some of the new cell phone applications. Many of the new phone apps are voice activated. One of the apps I like is a voice-activated search engine. This app has all the potential in the world to help me find the nearest shoe store, coffee house or anything else I am looking for, but it's powerless until I start to speak. Once I speak, the app hears my voice and performs the words I have spoken. Within seconds, a list of nearby shoe stores or coffee shops will pop up on my phone screen. My app is watching over my words to perform them.

The Lord is watching over His Word to perform it. Why not activate His Word with your voice today? Then, watch as He puts on a well-timed, customized, God-ordained, grand performance in your life.

Start the voice activation by saying, "Just like Jeremiah, according to God's Word, I can do all things through Christ who strengthens me."

False Humility

When I was a young Christian in my early twenties, I had a good friend named John. Johnny and I would have breakfast about once a week to talk about what God was doing in our lives. We both felt called by God to some sort of ministry, so it was always so encouraging to visit with John. (Today, John serves as a minister of helps for the senior pastor of a large, growing church in Michigan.)

Our conversations usually went something like this, "Hey Johnny, what's God doing in your life?"

Then he'd share a Scripture or something God had shown him, and he'd ask me, "Beth, what's God doing in your life?" and I would share something God had recently shown me. These conversations were a breath of fresh air.

Often, we'd talk about people we admired in ministry—the author of a book we'd read, our pastors or other preachers; we were always in such awe of these great people of God. I found myself sincerely trying to be humble by saying things like, "Yeah, so-and-so is awesome. I could never do what they are doing. I could never see myself doing those types of things. They are so gifted and amazing. I can't imagine being used by God like that."

One day, as I left our breakfast meeting, the Lord spoke to my heart and said, "Quit saying that. Quit it because you're developing faith in your inability. You are going to need my ability to do what I've called you to do, so don't develop faith in your inability." I instantly understood what He was saying, and I immediately quit making those "I-could-never-do" comments.

Sometimes, in our attempts to be humble, we end up with a false humility by saying things that contradict the Word of God. True biblical humility is to see ourselves as

God sees us and say what God says about us—we are not to think more highly nor more lowly of ourselves than we ought. We need to think and speak of ourselves in line with God's Word.

Decree It

If we want to please the Lord with our faith, we should boldly declare the truth of God's Word. We need to declare what God has said about us so He can perform His Word in our lives.

Many of us have not even scratched the surface of this powerful truth. God has endowed man with one of the most amazing gifts and honors—the ability to speak words that have the power of life or death. When we decide upon something in line with God's Word and we decree it, it will be established for us: "You shall also decide and decree a thing, and it shall be established for you; and the light [of God's favor] shall shine upon your ways," (Job 22:28 AMP).

Do you need some help priming the decree-it pump? Go ahead. With true humility and godly boldness, proclaim these in-Christ realities over your life. Remember, God is watching over His Word to perform it. It's time to decree it:

I decree Jesus is the Lord of my life. I live to please the Lord and know Jesus more intimately.

I decree Jesus is my Redeemer. He has redeemed me from sin to eternal life, from sickness to health and healing, from poverty and lack to abundance and blessing.

I decree the favor of God surrounds me like a shield. I have favor with God and man. I like people, and they like me.

I decree I am filled with peace. I am easygoing and patient.

I decree I am accepted in Christ. God loves me, and He's made me righteous in His sight without any sense of guilt, inferiority or shame.

I decree I can do all things through Christ who strengthens me. I can do all that God asks of me.

I decree my spouse and kids are blessed. We are a family mightily used of God.

I decree the joy of the Lord is my strength. I am happy and full of joy and laughter.

I decree I am blessed to be a blessing. I am generous and consider it a joy to bless others.

I decree I am a witness for the Lord. I love God and serve others. My life shines as a light for Jesus.

I decree I am fearfully and wonderfully made. My confidence is in the Lord.

I decree I love Him because He first loved me. I love God, and I love people.

I decree I have the mind of Christ. God has not given me a spirit of fear but of love, power and a sound mind.

I decree because I have set my love upon the Lord, He will satisfy me with a long life.

I decree the Greater One lives in me. Since God is for me, no one can successfully be against me.

I decree I did not choose Him, He chose me. I am ordained to bear fruit, much fruit, fruit that remains.

I decree I live for an audience of One. My purpose is to bring Him praise and glory in all that I am and all that I do.

As you boldly declare and decree God's Word, may His eyes find you, and may He put on a grand performance in and through your life.

CHAPTER 10

The Good Life

Blessed to be a blessing: I think that is one of the best summaries of the Christian life. Loved to love. Forgiven to forgive. Understood to understand. Encouraged to encourage. Blessed to be a blessing. God wants us to live blessed lives so we can be a blessing to others. It's a simple truth, yet many people are not living this blessed life. Why? Interestingly, there is only one major stumbling block to the good life—our mouths.

Want Good Days?

The Lord has promised us the potential for a blessed life—a life full of good days.

> He who would love life and see good days, let him refrain his tongue from evil, and his lips from speaking deceit. Let him turn away from evil and do good; let him seek peace and pursue it. For the eyes of the Lord are on the righteous, and His ears

are open to their prayers; but the face of the Lord is against those who do evil.

1 Peter 3:10-12

Do you see the connection between our words and good days? Let's read 1 Peter 3:10 in a few different versions of the Bible:

"Whoever wants to embrace life and see the day fill up with good, here's what you do: say nothing evil or hurtful," (MSG).

"For let him who wants to enjoy life and see good days [good—whether apparent or not] keep his tongue free from evil and his lips from guile (treachery, deceit)," (AMP).

"If you want to enjoy life and see many happy days, keep your tongue from speaking evil, and your lips from telling lies," (NLT).

This may be one of the Word's best-kept secrets. Unfortunately, we live in a put-down culture. People like to push each other down. We live in a sarcastic, dog-eat-dog, every-man-for-himself culture where people get elected, get promoted, get laughs and make money by hurting others. God's way is different. If we want to enjoy life and see good days, we must carefully guard our mouths.

Don't Be Hating

Sarcasm was one of the first things God dealt with me on as a baby Christian. Like many people, I grew up in an environment where sarcastic humor was one of the primary ways we communicated with others. We usually had fun by being sarcastic, but often our remarks were caustic and had subtle digs in them. I didn't know what 1 Peter 3:10 said at the time. I didn't realize the Lord was trying to set me up for a good life by helping me put a guard on my mouth; but that's exactly what He was doing.

If we want to love life and see good days, we can't put people down. We can't be a part of saying bad things about people. We must not gossip. We can't justify saying hurtful words. We need to return to the adage our mothers taught us, "If you can't say something nice, don't say anything at all."

My husband and I have been the senior pastors of a growing church for over eighteen years, and sadly we've seen sarcasm, put-downs, criticism, evil speaking, lies and loose talking aren't just a problem outside of the church walls; it's a problem inside the church too. For some reason, people seem to think they can get away with talking any way they want with no repercussions.

We've received plenty of very nice, encouraging notes over the years; but we are always surprised when we receive an especially mean-spirited note or e-mail, not because we think we are perfect or past making improvements but because we are surprised that people have the nerve to be so vicious with their words. We often wonder if they realize the damage they are doing to their own lives by speaking such words? It's definitely not the recipe for seeing good days.

Many people could instantly see good days if they would clean up their words as they relate to what they say about spiritual authorities. The Lord does not condone or appreciate it when anyone speaks evil of those He has placed in positions of authority—in particular, spiritual authority. We live in a culture that encourages people to express their disagreements and criticisms. People feel entitled to make opinionated comments about TV preachers, Christian leaders, pastors and other God-ordained leaders, as if God were not listening. He is.

Have you ever read what happened to Aaron and Miriam when they spoke against Moses? (Num. 12:1-15.) How about Korah, Dathan and Abiram when they stirred up the whole congregation with their words and spoke against Moses? (Num. 16:1-50.) If you want to love life and see good days, don't come against God's anointed leaders with your words. If you have an issue with a Christian leader or someone who is over you in the Lord, if possible, talk to them in private, pray and leave that person in God's hands; it is in your best interest to do so.

Keep Your Tongue

If we want to love life and see good days, what does the Bible say about the things we should and shouldn't say? Here are a few Scriptures to meditate on.

Be nice: "Get rid of all bitterness, rage and anger, brawling and slander, along with every form of malice. Be kind and compassionate to one another, forgiving each other, just as in Christ God forgave you," (Eph. 4:31,32 NIV).

Uproot bitterness: "See to it that no one misses the grace of God and that no bitter root grows up to cause trouble and defile many," (Heb. 12:15 NIV).

Wear new clothes: "But now you must rid yourselves of all such things as these: anger, rage, malice, slander, and filthy language from your lips. Do not lie to each other, since you have taken off your old self with its practices and have put on the new self, which is being renewed in knowledge in the image of its Creator. . . . Therefore, as God's chosen people, holy and dearly loved, clothe yourselves with compassion, kindness, humility, gentleness and patience. Bear with each other and forgive whatever grievances you may have against one another. Forgive as the Lord forgave you. And over all these virtues put on love, which binds them all together in perfect unity," (Col. 3:8-10; 12-14 NIV).

Say goodbye: "Therefore, rid yourselves of all malice and all deceit, hypocrisy, envy, and slander of every kind," (1 Pet. 2:1 NIV).

If we want to love life and see good days, we must get a grip on our lip.

If you want to love life and see good days, don't speak evil about yourself.

One other thing, most of us know we should be careful about the things we say to or about others, but what about the things we say to or about ourselves? Don't hate yourself. We live in a culture of extremes. People are either so in love with themselves they become narcissists, or they hate themselves and become overly self-deprecating. On one hand, it's wise and healthy to not think more highly of yourself than you ought and to not take yourself quite so seriously; but on the other hand, if you constantly insult yourself, you may start to believe what you say. If you want to love life and see good days, don't speak evil about yourself.

The Evil Report

God takes our words very seriously, especially when our words are evil and contradict His Word. If we want to see good days, we must keep our tongue from evil. Let's look at another angle on evil words.

There is an important story in the Old Testament. The Lord promised a good land—appropriately called the Promised Land—to Moses and the people of Israel, but in order to enjoy this land, they were going to have to go in and possess it. As part of their strategic possession plan, the Lord told Moses' spies to scope out the Promised Land prior to their entrance. Moses obeyed, and twelve spies were sent out to do reconnaissance. When they returned, they gave this report:

> And Caleb stilled the people before Moses, and said, "Let us go up at once, and possess it; for we are well able to overcome it."
>
> But the men that went up with him said, "We be not able to go up against the people; for they are stronger than we."
>
> And they brought up an evil report of the land which they had searched unto the children of Israel, saying, "The land, through which we have gone to search it, is a land that eateth up the inhabitants thereof; and all the people that we saw in it are men of a great stature.
>
> And there we saw the giants, the sons of Anak, which come of the giants: and we were in our own sight as grasshoppers, and so we were in their sight."
>
> Numbers 13:30-33 KJV

Two of the spies, Caleb and Joshua, came back with a good report; and ten of the spies returned from their assignment with an evil report. In due season, Caleb and Joshua possessed the Promised Land while the ten spies who brought an evil report died from a plague. Here's what happened:

And the men, which Moses sent to search the land, who returned, and made all the congregation to murmur against him, by bringing up a slander upon the land,

Even those men that did bring up the evil report upon the land, died by the plague before the Lord.

But Joshua the son of Nun, and Caleb the son of Jephunneh, which were of the men that went to search the land, lived still.

Numbers 14:36-38 KJV

At first glance, when we read the story of the ten spies and their report, it doesn't sound evil—it just sounds like human anxiety. However, God considered their words to be evil. Why? He expects His people to live in agreement with His Word by faith, not by sight. From the Lord's view, their report was equivalent to speaking evil, and the result was they didn't get to love life and see good days. Instead, their words opened the door for them to die by the plague.

Joshua and Caleb, on the other hand, returned with a good report. They said, "We are well able to take it. Let's go up at once and possess the land." They ended up opening the door for loving life and seeing good days for their families and them. They were the only ones who entered the Promised Land.

If you want to love life and see good days, keep your tongue from speaking evil.

Speaking the Truth in Love

Let's conclude this chapter with a short discussion on the importance of speaking the truth in love. In some situations, we need to speak words that the listener may not want to hear; we may need to share words of correction, admonition or rebuke. It's our job to speak words in love and pray that the recipient has ears to hear.

When we speak the truth, it helps people grow up: "But, speaking the truth in love, may grow up in all things into Him who is the head—Christ," (Eph. 4:15). When we rebuke a wise person, he will be wiser:

> Do not correct a scoffer, lest he hate you; rebuke a wise man, and he will love you. Give instruction to a wise man, and he will be still wiser; teach a just man, and he will increase in learning.
>
> Proverbs 9:8,9

Speaking the truth in love in a gracious way is an art. We need the Lord's help to speak words that cause others to learn and grow. These two passages set the bar for us as we speak good words:

> A word fitly spoken is like apples of gold in settings of silver. Like an earring of gold and an ornament of fine gold is a wise rebuker to an obedient ear.
>
> Proverbs 25:11,12

"The wise in heart will be called prudent, and sweetness of the lips increases learning."

Proverbs 16:21

CHAPTER 11:

Little Mouth— Big Words

Horses, boats, fires, mankind—what do they all have in common? They are directed by little things. For the horse, it's a bit. For the boat, it's a rudder. For the fire, it's a spark. For mankind, it's our tongues.

Metaphors

In the book of James, our little tongues are compared to several big metaphors. Let's take a look.

For we all stumble in many things. If anyone does not stumble in word, he is a perfect man, able also to bridle the whole body. Indeed, we put bits in horses' mouths that they may obey us, and we turn their whole body. Look also at ships: although they are so large and are driven by fierce winds, they are turned by a very small rudder wherever the pilot desires.

Even so the tongue is a little member and boasts great things. See how great a forest a little fire kindles! And the tongue is a fire, a world of iniquity. The tongue is so set among our members that it defiles the whole body, and sets on fire the course of nature; and it is set on fire by hell. For every kind of beast and bird, of reptile and creature of the sea, is tamed and has been tamed by mankind. But no man can tame the tongue. It is an unruly evil, full of deadly poison. With it we bless our God and Father, and with it we curse men, who have been made in the similitude of God. Out of the same mouth proceed blessing and cursing. My brethren, these things ought not to be so. Does a spring send forth fresh water and bitter from the same opening? Can a fig tree, my brethren, bear olives, or a grapevine bear figs? Thus no spring yields both salt water and fresh.

James 3:2-12

The Big Horse and the Little Bit

A big horse is controlled with a little bit in his mouth. If the horse wanted to, he could buck off any rider and go wherever he wanted to go, but the bit in his mouth turns his whole body around. In the same way, our little tongues can turn things around in our lives. Do you need a turnaround?

Specifically, you can turn your whole body around with your tongue. If your body is facing some physical challenges, one way to start turning your whole body around is with words. As you get your mouth into agreement with God and His Word, things can turn. Look at Psalm 103:2-5:

> Bless the Lord, O my soul, and forget not all His benefits: Who forgives all your iniquities, Who heals all your diseases, Who redeems your life from destruction, Who crowns you with lovingkindness and tender mercies, Who satisfies your mouth with good things, so that your youth is renewed like the eagle's.

Like the bit in the horse's mouth, you can speak this passage of Scripture over your life, and in time, things will begin to turn. With the bit of your tongue, you say, "He forgives all my sins and heals all of my diseases. He redeems my life. He crowns me with His tender mercies. He satisfies me with good things. He renews my youth," and then you trust the Lord to do what only He can do. He may heal you supernaturally; He may connect you to a new doctor; He may lead you to change some of your dietary habits. He will help you follow whatever pathway is needed to heal your diseases, renew your youth and turn your whole body around.

The Big Ship and the Little Rudder

A very small rudder drives the ship. The pilot sets the course and steers that big ship using the small rudder. The captain determines which port or destination he wants to reach, and he sets the rudder to hit that destination. He will not be deterred by wind or waves. Even so, the tongue is a little member in light of your whole body, but it directs the course of your life.

Let's say the pilot starts in Port A, but he wants to get to Port B. That pilot will have to factor in the wind and waves and adjust his rudder in order to compensate for those challenges; but in due time, that rudder will direct him to Port B.

When we set our tongues in the direction of God's plan and destiny for our lives, we'll eventually get there. If we are in Port A but know God wants us to move to Port B, we need to set our words in the direction of Port B. As we start to sail, we may need to factor in challenges and obstacles we will face and recalibrate the rudders of our tongues to compensate for these things. It may take time, even years or decades, but at the right time, we will arrive at Port B.

Boston University: I remember one of the first times I applied this passage of Scripture to my life. I was nineteen years old and living in Port W as a college student at Western Michigan University. I was the assistant director of my dorm and a biology major who wanted to be a dentist. During this time, God dramatically interrupted my life and called me to the ministry.

By faith, I understood I needed to transfer from Port W to Port B to attend Boston University. I knew I had to launch out onto the sea of faith. Immediately, I could see a few big waves that posed challenges as I thought about moving from Port W to Port B. First, Boston University was a private school in another state and about eight times more expensive than WMU. Second, as the assistant director of the dorm at Western, I had a paid position that came in handy as a college student. I would be giving that up to transfer. Third, I planned to change universities, switch my major from biology to communications, not lose any credits and still graduate in four years. (This would require a working of miracles!) Fourth, I wanted to transfer in the middle of my junior year in college. Fifth, I wanted the majority of my education to be funded with scholarships and grants, and I preferred either no loans or very small loans.

I knew all things are possible with God (Phil. 4:13), so I put my trust in Him and began to set my rudder for Port B. My first step was to apply. I did, and I was accepted and could enroll as a student in January 1980. The next thing I needed to do was complete all of the financial-aid forms. The financial-aid office at BU was not very encouraging when they informed me that as a transfer student who was from out of state and transferring in the middle of the year, my chances of getting scholarships and grants would be slim since most of those funds had already been given to students at the beginning of the school year. They promised to look at all of my forms and run me through their computer grids to see what they could do, but they were not hopeful. I was not deterred.

In August 1979, with my acceptance to BU intact, my boat was free to sail; so I held my rudder and began to say, "God is bigger than the BU computer system." (In my mind and heart the computer system included everyone involved with financial aid.)

In September of '79, I returned to Western Michigan University to finish up the fall semester and prepare to transfer to Boston for the winter semester in January of '80. In October of '79, I began to call the Boston University financial aid office to see about the status of my financial aid. I distinctly remember speaking with a young lady named Julie. Over the next few months, we got to know each other on a first-name basis. Each time I called, Julie would tell me they didn't have any information for me. The board had not met, and the powers-that-be had not made a decision. I continued to hold the rudder steady as I said, "God is bigger than the BU computer system."

By late November '79, several things were happening on the WMU campus. First, everyone was registering for winter classes—everyone except me. I did not register for classes because I had set my rudder, and I knew, one way or another, I was going to Port B—Boston University. Drops and ads came and went, and I still was not registered to be an ongoing student at WMU. The second thing that came up concerned my job as the assistant director of the dorm. I knew I needed to let my boss know I would be leaving at Christmas break so they could replace me.

By December '79, I still had not heard any official word from BU. When Christmas break came, I resigned from my job in the dorm, said goodbye to my friends and moved off campus to return home; still, no word from BU. I continued to say, "God is bigger than the BU computer system." I called Julie every day during Christmas break. "Has your board met? Will I receive the scholarships and grants?" Time after time, Julie responded with,

"No, they haven't met. We don't know anything."

I kept my rudder set: "God is bigger than the BU computer system."

Over Christmas break, my best friend, Michelle, who was a student at Boston College (down the street from Boston University), and I were making plans to drive to Boston together so she could return to school and so I could move into an apartment near Boston U. I continued to call Julie, and she continued to tell me they didn't know anything. I held fast to my confession of faith; the rudder was set: "God is bigger than the BU computer system."

Several days before our proposed departure, by faith, Michelle and I packed our things in her car in preparation of the big move. Still I had not heard any definitive word from BU.

Two days before we going to drive to Boston, I called Julie. "Hey Julie, this is Beth. How's it going? How are the kids? (We were practically best friends by now.) Do you have any information for me?"

She said, "You got it. You got your financial aid—all of it!" I was thrilled and thankful.

Indeed, God was bigger than the BU computer system—bigger than all the board members, all the forms and all the odds stacked against me.

We drove to Boston. I arrived at Port B and attended Boston University. I earned my Bachelor of Science in Communications within the four-year timeframe I had desired, and I ended up paying less money out of pocket to attend the prestigious, private Boston University than I would have paid by working in the dorms and attending WMU.

Only God could pull something like that off—and He did—by faith and the power of that little rudder— my tongue.

So, what about you? Which port are you in these days? Which port does the Lord have in mind for you?

If you're currently single, let me encourage you with another story and exciting faith adventure.

They All Want Me—Bad! I was single and in my mid-twenties. I was living in what we will call Port S—single, but I really wanted to be in Port M—married.

I am the oldest of four sisters, so you have to appreciate the pain I suffered during a two-year period when I was a bridesmaid in five weddings. When my youngest sister, Michelle, got engaged and married, I was in her wedding—a beautiful black, white and red affair. Then, my third-oldest sister, Kelly, got engaged and married. I was in her wedding—a stunning navy-blue theme. Then, my second oldest sister, Rhonda, got engaged and married. I was in her wedding—a lovely yellow color scheme. Then, my two best friends Michelle and Mary Jo both got engaged, and I was in their weddings. I can honestly say I was happy for all my sisters and my two friends, but I was getting really discouraged being "always the bridesmaid and never the bride." The worst part was when I looked on the dating landscape, I didn't see anyone on the horizon. I was stuck in Port S.

Eventually, after many tears, I realized in addition to the normal course of working at my job, growing in the Lord and living my life, I had to seek the Lord and reset my rudder if I wanted to get to Port M. I had to get my words working in the right direction.

I began to seek the Lord. "God," I said, "what's the deal on marriage? I'm ready to meet the man of my dreams. Lord, where is he?" I was earnestly praying, "God, where is the man of my dreams? I pray he's been born and is alive and well on earth somewhere. I can't wait around forever."

As I was praying and seeking the Lord, I discovered this verse, which was like manna from heaven,

Search from the book of the Lord, and read: Not one of these shall fail; Not one shall lack her mate.

For My mouth has commanded it, and His Spirit has gathered them.

Isaiah 34:16

When I read that verse of Scripture, I knew this was my rhema word for Port M.

So, I set my rudder and started saying that verse. "The Spirit of the Lord is gathering us. He's gathering my spouse and me. None shall lack their mate." I believed it. I said it. However, I began to notice a crosswind blowing against me. The winds that were blowing against me were my own insecurities. I was struggling with the idea that anyone would want me. I wondered, *Are there any men left? Will anybody want me?*

The winds were blowing against me, and the enemy was whispering in my ear, "No one's going to want you; you'll be 100 years old by the time you find somebody. Do you remember the card game Old Maid™? That's going to be you!" I could see this was definitely going to be a fight of a faith.

I continued to say what God said, "The Spirit of the Lord is gathering us. He's gathering my spouse and me. None shall lack their mate." I also realized I needed to reset my rudder to compensate for the wind.

I prayed, "Lord, I need a phrase. I need an extreme phrase because strong winds are blowing. I believe Your Word, 'none shall lack their mate,' and that includes me. I need more power to set this rudder of mine against the winds of discouragement trying to blow me off course. What else should I say?"

As I pondered this, I knew for my own sake I would have to be a little dramatic. After thinking for a while, suddenly this phrase came into my heart, "They all want me—bad!"

It was such an over-the-top phrase, I laughed, but then I embraced it. I decided this would be my new phrase and my response to the devil's lies. When those whispers came to my mind, "No one will ever want you," I just said,

"They all want me, and they all want me—bad!" I started to say that every day, every hour when necessary.

To be honest, when I first started saying this phrase, I didn't feel like it was true. I just said it by faith. But, over time, something happened. I actually started to believe my words. The Bible says, "Faith comes by hearing"; so the more I said it, the more I believed "they all want me—bad!" Within a few months, I sensed my boat had sailed through those crosswinds, and by faith, I could see Port M coming into view. I fully expected Mr. Wonderful to come along and want me—bad!

Then one fine day, he walked into my life, and I met my beloved, Jeff Jones. We started to date, and within a short time, we knew because we knew because we knew that the Lord had "gathered" us. We were compatible; we enjoyed being together; we loved to laugh; and we both had a passion to serve the Lord. It was truly a match made in heaven.

The icing on the cake was a conversation Jeff and I had while we were engaged. One day, he looked at me and said, "I want you—bad!" I couldn't believe it. He didn't even know about my dramatic little phrase. I smiled and gave a little shout out to the Lord, "Okay, Lord, I get it—it works!"

We were married in Port M one year later, and now nearly twenty-five years and four kids later, he still wants me—bad! (I, too, want him—bad!)

So, what about you? Have you set your rudder to the port God desires for you? Things may not change or happen overnight, but if you'll be strong in faith and consistent in setting your rudder according to God's Word, at the proper time, you will arrive at your desired destination.

The Big Fire and the Little Spark

The Bible also describes our tongues with the metaphor of a spark. A big fire is started by a tiny spark. Our little tongues can spark big fires—fires of strife, division and trouble. Starting gossip fires has become a part of our media-frenzied culture, "Scoundrels hunt for scandal; their words are a destructive blaze," (Prov. 16:27 NLT). That's why we need the Lord's help to tame our tongues.

Proverbs also gives us a great piece of wisdom for putting fires out,

Where there is no wood, the fire goes out; and where there is no talebearer, strife ceases. As charcoal is to burning coals, and wood to fire, so is a contentious man to kindle strife.

Proverbs 26:20,21

If we want to steer clear of starting or fueling fires, we need to quit putting wood on them. Where there is no wood, the fire goes out. Anytime you are being drawn into an undesired conversation, an argument, contention or strife, there is one quick way to bring it to a halt. Don't throw any wood on the fire. Our flesh is tempted to get in the last word, to give people a piece of our minds or to fully explain ourselves, but sometimes the wisest thing to do is be quiet. If we will guard our mouths and not allow words to add fuel to any fires, those damaging fires will go out. Where there is no wood, the fire goes out.

In conclusion, be sure to take time to give consideration to the power of your tongue as it relates to the bit in a horse's mouth, the rudder on a big ship and the spark that starts big fires; and ask the Lord to help you tame your tongue appropriately.

CHAPTER 12

A Woman with Issues

Got issues? Jesus worked miracles for a woman with an issue. That means there's hope for all of us. These days, He's still helping women—and men—with issues. Let's take a look at this story and see what role her words played in her miraculous healing:

> And a certain woman, which had an issue of blood twelve years, and had suffered many things of many physicians, and had spent all that she had, and was nothing bettered, but rather grew worse, when she had heard of Jesus, came in the press behind, and touched his garment. For she said, "If I may touch but his clothes, I shall be whole." And straightway the fountain of her blood was dried up; and she felt in her body that she was healed of that plague.
>
> And Jesus, immediately knowing in himself that virtue had gone out of him, turned him about in the press, and said, "Who touched my clothes?"

And his disciples said unto him, "Thou seest the multitude thronging thee, and sayest thou, 'Who touched me?'"

And he looked round about to see her that had done this thing. But the woman fearing and trembling, knowing what was done in her, came and fell down before him, and told him all the truth. And he said unto her, "Daughter, thy faith hath made thee whole; go in peace, and be whole of thy plague."

Mark 5:25-34 KJV

Do you have any issues? Your words of faith will play a vital role in God's ability to work in your life. Let's break this story down to see what role the woman's words played.

Twelve Years

This was a real woman—a certain woman. We don't know her name. We only know her as "the woman with the issue of blood." We know she has suffered many things for twelve years. She has an issue of blood. Her issue is messy. It is embarrassing. It is humiliating. Some Bible versions call it a flow of blood or a hemorrhage. For twelve years, she lives with a messy, embarrassing, humiliating issue.

Twelve years is a long time. She dealt with this issue from the time her firstborn started school until he graduated from high school. What was her life like for those twelve years? She probably couldn't volunteer at the Valentine's Day party for her fourth grader. She probably couldn't sit in the bleachers and watch her daughter play volleyball, and she couldn't cheer her son on in basketball. She probably couldn't go golfing with her husband. I doubt she went shopping at the mall with her girlfriends. I'll bet she couldn't attend church or synagogue or volunteer to serve in preschool. She probably couldn't sit at Starbucks™ and have a coffee with a friend. They were probably a lot of things she couldn't do. Why? Because she had an issue.

What about you? Do you have any issues hindering you from experiencing life? Have you had an issue for a long time? Perhaps you've experienced a chronic illness or a pattern of broken relationships or various addictions or a life of sadness and depression. No matter what the issue is and no matter how long you've experienced it, Jesus is still the same, and He can help you.

Her Identity and Despair

Notice, this woman became identified with her issue. We don't even know her name. We only know her as "the woman with the issue of blood." (Really, if the truth were known, she should be known as the woman healed of the issue of blood.) She became identified with her issue, and a lot of times that happens to us. We get so identified with our issues we can't imagine our lives free from them.

For example, if you've been divorced, maybe that has become your identity. If you've faced some dramatic or traumatic experience in your life, that can become your identity. If you've experienced a failure or embarrassment or if you have engaged in something that has filled you with shame, that may become your identity until Jesus comes on the scene.

This woman had suffered many things of many physicians. She went to all the doctors. She went to the Jerusalem Clinic and to the John Hopkins of Galilee; she went to all the best doctors, and they couldn't help her. In fact, she got worse.

Doctors are wonderful, but sometimes doctors cannot help us. Sometimes we face situations that no other human being can fix. Sometimes, the doctors can't heal us. The government can't help us. Education can't improve us. Mom and Dad can't make it all better. Your best friend can't fix it. Some issues cause us to have our backs up against a wall desperate for God.

If you're facing a situation that seems to be going from bad to worse, be encouraged. Things can change!

That's where this woman was. The doctors couldn't help her, and she was getting worse; not only that, she had spent all the money she had. She was still sick and broke.

If you're facing a situation that seems to be going from bad to worse, be encouraged. Things can change!

Hearing, Believing and Speaking

This woman began to hear about Jesus, and faith came into her heart: "When she had heard of Jesus, she came behind Him in the crowd and touched His garment. For she said, 'If only I may touch His clothes, I shall be made well,'" (Mark 5:27,28).

What did she hear? She must have heard God had anointed this man with power and with the Holy Spirit, and He went about doing good and healing everybody that had been afflicted by the devil. She must have heard and heard and heard all about Jesus, and she must have believed what she heard. The words she heard must have gotten into her heart in abundance. How do we know that? Because from the abundance of the heart, the mouth speaks (Matt. 12:34); and the next thing we know, this woman started to say something.

She said to herself, *If I can touch that man's garment, I know I will be healed.* Listen to what it says in the *Amplified Bible,* "For she kept saying to herself, 'If I only touch His garment, I shall be restored to health,'" (Matt. 9:21). I imagine she muttered that phrase over and over.

Here's what she didn't say. She didn't say, "Why me? This is so unfair." She didn't say, "Fine. I'll try this Jesus stuff. If it's God's will, He'll heal me." She didn't say, "Hey, you never know. Maybe this faith stuff works."

She did say, "If I only touch his garment, I shall be restored to health." She heard about Jesus' ministry, and it got big in her heart; and then out of the abundance of her heart, she spoke words of faith.

Sometimes people think they can try the words thing. They'll say things like, "Yeah, I tried that words thing once. I was depressed for ten years, so I said 'I'm happy. The joy of the Lord is my strength' twice. It didn't work for me. I'm still depressed." Listen, it's going to take more than two times. You might have to say something for weeks. You might have to say something for months. If you've experienced an issue for years, it's going to take some time to hear about Jesus, allow faith in Him to get big in your heart and then out of the abundance of your heart you will speak as long as it takes.

Healed, Healthy and Whole

So, what happened to the woman? Jesus healed her. This woman with the issue of blood was not going to take no for an answer. She was determined. She engaged her faith with her mouth. She put the law of words to work. The result? The Bible says, "Straightway the fountain of her blood was dried up," (v. 29).

Her faith activated the healing power of Jesus. The Bible says Jesus looked at the crowd and said, "Who touched me?" He knew that someone with faith was in the vicinity, and that person's faith caused the healing anointing to flow from Him into that person's issue. When Jesus saw this woman, He said, "Daughter, your faith has made you well," (Mark 5:34).

That should be a big encouragement to all of us. Today, our faith can do the same thing for us. Jesus is the same yesterday, today and forever; so if He healed a woman with an issue yesterday, He will heal anyone with an issue today.

If you're facing an issue, do what the woman with the issue of blood did. Seek whatever natural, medical help is available. Take time to hear from Jesus and see what the Word says about your issue. Hear it over and over. Read the Bible passages that are pertinent to your issue over and over. Faith will come. Once faith fills your heart in abundance, begin to speak. Say within yourself what you know to be true. Say what you believe. Activate your faith with your words. God's power will go to work on your behalf, and Jesus will heal and deliver you from any and all issues.

CHAPTER 13:

What Not To Say

Have you ever seen the show, *What Not to Wear*™? Two sharp, witty and smartly dressed hosts help people discover their best style. They usually start by going through the closets and wardrobe of the show's participants; immediately they begin to discard ratty old clothes that are out of style. They spend a bit of time teaching people what *not* to wear, and then they really go to work helping them discover the best styles to flatter the person's body shape. In the end, they learn what to wear in order to be their best.

We need the Holy Spirit's help going through the closet of our mouths to help us discard ratty, old words that should not be a part of our vocabulary.

In our lives, we often need a little dose of *What Not to Say*. Because we live in a culture that thinks it's entitled to say what it wants—completely free from any accountability or repercussions—we need the Holy Spirit's help going through the closet of our mouths to help us discard ratty, old words that should not be a part of our vocabulary.

"Shut Up!"—A Good Place to Start

In Matthew 6:31 KJV, Jesus says, "Therefore take no thought, saying, 'What shall we eat?' or, 'What shall we drink?'" In other words, Jesus explains the way we "take a thought" is by saying words. In this example, Jesus explains when our thoughts are full of anxiety or fear, we shouldn't bring those thoughts into reality by saying words. This is a kingdom principle. Words bring thoughts into the tangible realm. Therefore, sometimes the best thing to do is shut up!

If negative thoughts come to you, and you're not sure what God's Word says to you about it, don't say anything. Wait until you have some understanding from the Lord before speaking—take no thought saying anything else. We don't have to give a voice to our thoughts, and often we are much better off if we don't.

On the other hand, what if we do want to take a thought? If we look at the reverse application of this verse, we discover we can take hold of a good God-thought by saying it.

Let's say these thoughts come to you: *You can do it. God wants you to succeed. He didn't create you to fail. If God is for you, who can be against you?* Let's say you want to own these thoughts, so what do you do? You say them. You take the thoughts by saying. Open your mouth, and say those thoughts out loud. In fact, that's exactly what Jesus said in Luke 17:6, "If you have faith as a mustard seed, you can say." We can take a faith-thought by saying.

I found the 2009 special issue of *U.S. News and World Report* on "Secrets of the Super Rich" interesting. It stated the super rich—people who win—are careful with their thoughts, and they don't say, "I can't do that" or "it's too risky" or "I can't afford it"; instead they say, "How can I do that?" or "How can I reduce my risk?" or "How can I afford it?"

Successful people have discovered the biblical principle and importance of not voicing their negative thoughts with words. They've learned to apply the two things Jesus said. Don't take a negative thought by saying. Do take a faith-filled thought by saying.

Turn Off the Flow

Notice what the writer of Proverbs said, "When words are many, sin is not absent, but he who holds his tongue is wise," (10:19 NIV). This is a clear admonition to those of us who are tempted to run at the mouth with empty words. What type of words fall into this "many" category?

Many words are empty and void of substance.

Many words are full of anger, bitterness and resentment.

Many words are full of pride, ego and an it's-all-about-me attitude.

Many words are arrogant rants, selfish tantrums or opinionated outbursts.

Many words are insensitive, hurtful, critical and damaging.

Many words carry a patronizing, self-righteous tone of condescension.

Many words are out of place, inappropriate or lacking in judgment.

How do you avoid talking too much? Turn off the flow! The *New Living Translation* makes it plain, "Don't talk too much, for it fosters sin. Be sensible and turn off the flow!" (Prov. 10:19).

Let Your Words Be Few

The writer of Ecclesiastes cuts to the chase,

Do not be rash with your mouth, and let not your heart utter anything hastily before God. For God is in heaven, and you on earth; therefore let your words be few. For a dream comes through much activity, and a fool's voice is known by his many words.

Ecclesiastes 5:2,3

Once again, we are admonished to avoid empty, rash, hasty words. This is a good rule of thumb especially if our words are going to do more harm than good.

James had it right: "Everyone should be quick to listen, slow to speak and slow to become angry," (James 1:19 NIV). Are people running from you? Not answering your calls? Avoiding contact? Have you ever asked why? Perhaps, it's a word problem. Why not "be slow to speak" for a season, and see what happens?

No More Potty Mouth

A few years ago, I followed a few pastors on Twitter™; later I had to unfollow them because of their constant use of the phrase "holy crap." I couldn't reconcile the idea of a spiritual leader being so comfortable in using this combination of words on a regular basis. In fact, this Twitter™ situation made me evaluate my own choice of words.

The Holy Spirit, through the apostle Paul, told us what type of words we need to delete: "Obscene stories, foolish talk, and coarse jokes—these are not for you. Instead, let there be thankfulness to God," (Eph. 5:4 NLT).

These days, people are very loose with their words. That's just the way of the world, but that shouldn't be the way of a Christ follower, should it? Words are tools, and they can do so much to encourage, strengthen, refresh, exhort and correct people. We need to use them in wise, creative, relevant and redemptive ways.

Have you done a words inventory lately? It might not hurt—or then again—it might hurt a lot! Here are some things to consider.

Words Can Grieve the Holy Spirit: I don't know about you, but I don't want to grieve or sadden the Holy Spirit. I need all the help He will give me. I need His anointing to speak, write and do what He's called me to do; so the laugh or attention I might get by using unwholesome words is not worth grieving the Holy Spirit. "Do not let any unwholesome talk come out of your mouths, but only what is helpful for building others up according to their needs, that it may benefit those who listen. And do not grieve the Holy Spirit of God," (Eph. 4:29,30 NIV).

Words Can Get You in Trouble: Ever heard of someone who was "hung by the tongue"? Words can get us into trouble. Sometimes, we're the cause of our own trouble—wrecked relationships, demotion on the job, wayward kids or financial ruin—simply because we lacked discipline with our words. It's a high price to pay: "A man of perverse heart does not prosper; he whose tongue is deceitful falls into trouble," (Prov. 17:20 NIV).

Words Reveal a Rebellious Streak: Ever been considered a rebel? Sometimes, we use words out of pure rebellion—we swear, use carnal words or off-color phrases just to get attention or be funny. Being rebellious will never take us where we want to go. Besides that, our hearts know when we are being rebellious; we need to call ourselves out and make a decision to quit using certain words that feed that bit of rebellion. "The upright speak what is helpful; the wicked speak rebellion," (Prov. 10:32 TLB).

Let this be your prayer: "Post a guard at my mouth, God, set a watch at the door of my lips," (Ps. 141:3 MSG).

Don't Sow Words of Discord

> God is love, but did you know there are seven things He hates—detests! There are six things the LORD hates—no, seven things he detests: haughty eyes, a lying tongue, hands that kill the innocent, a heart that plots evil, feet that race to do wrong, a false witness who pours out lies, a person who sows discord in a family.
>
> Proverbs 6:16-19 NLT

Notice the last thing mentioned: a person who sows discord among a family. In modern terms, we might call this type of person a "mouth" or a "critic" or "opinionated" or a "strong personality"—and none of these is a compliment. If we want to get on God's bad side, we should follow the path of one who sows discord.

When someone is involved in conversations, comments or behavior that promotes disagreement, strife, quarreling, dissension, contention, conflict, arguments, friction and disharmony, that's sowing discord. As pastors, my husband and I take strife and sowing discord very seriously in our church. From our inception, we've told our church family we will tolerate a lot of things. We will walk with them through thick and thin; we will extend mercy and grace along with love and patience as we all grow and mature; but the one thing we won't tolerate is strife and discord. It's extremely damaging to a church, and it causes division and confusion in the body of Christ. God hates it, and we hate it.

Is there a difference between a healthy disagreement and sowing discord? Sure. The Bible is full of both. Jonathan was in disagreement with his father, Saul, about the role of David. He handled his disagreement with honor, and the result was God honored him, protected him and blessed his children. (2 Sam. 9:1-9.) On the other hand, as we've already mentioned, Korah, Dathan and Abiram disagreed with Moses about the direction Moses was taking the Israelites. They stirred up a rebellion to turn people against Moses. The result? God's judgment fell, and an earthquake swallowed up everyone who participated in the discord. (Num.16:1-32.)

What can we learn from these examples? We must handle disagreements with honor, and we must not sow discord. At times, we may have to agree to disagree and then make a decision to button our lips so we don't plant seeds of strife.

Sowing discord can be the result of various situations. Perhaps these examples will help you recognize the tentacles of the temptation to sow discord in your life. Once you find it, run in the opposite direction.

When we don't like or agree with the decision made by someone over us—in our frustration—we may be tempted to sow seeds of strife.

When we feel entitled to something but are denied—in our presumption—we may be tempted to blow something out of proportion by sowing seeds of disharmony.

When we are offended because we weren't treated according to our expectations—in our hurt—we may decide to hurt others by sowing seeds of accusation.

When we think more highly of ourselves than we ought but others don't share this exaggerated opinion—in our arrogance—we may feel justified in giving everyone who will listen a piece of our mind as we sow seeds of division.

If you're tempted to sow discord—don't! God hates it, and there isn't one Bible example where it turns out well for the person who sows discord.

If someone tries to lure you into a net of discord—run! You don't want any of the consequences that come with the association of those who sow discord.

If you want to get on God's good side—pursue doing the right thing! "The way of the wicked is an abomination, extremely disgusting and shamefully vile to the Lord, but He loves him who pursues righteousness (moral and spiritual rectitude in every area and relation)," (Prov. 15:9 AMP).

You Can't Go North and South at the Same Time

Let's look at one final thing regarding what not to say: you can't go north and south at the same time.

> But no man can tame the tongue. It is an unruly evil, full of deadly poison. With it we bless our God and Father, and with it we curse men, who have been made in the similitude of God. Out of the same mouth proceed blessing and cursing. My brethren, these things ought not to be so. Does a spring send forth fresh water and bitter from the same opening? Can a fig tree, my brethren, bear olives, or a grapevine bear figs? Thus no spring yields both salt water and fresh.
>
> Who is wise and understanding among you? Let him show by good conduct that his works are done in the meekness of wisdom. But if you have bitter envy and self-seeking in your hearts, do not boast and lie against the truth. This wisdom does not descend from above, but is earthly, sensual, demonic. For where envy and self-seeking exist, confusion and every evil thing are there. But the wisdom that is from above is first pure, then peaceable, gentle, willing to yield, full of mercy and good fruits, without partiality and without hypocrisy. Now the fruit of righteousness is sown in peace by those who make peace.
>
> James 5:8-18

It's oxymoronic for any Christian to bless God and curse men, to speak fresh words and bitter, to be a Christian and voice ungodly words. Make a decision to bless, to speak fresh words and to produce godly fruit with your words. James summarized it well when he said, "Out of the same mouth proceed blessing and cursing. My brethren, these things ought not to be so," (v. 10).

CHAPTER 14:

Talk with Your Mouth Full

God wants us to talk with our mouths full—full of His Word, full of faith, full of good fruit and full of thanks and praise. There is no doubt "the mouth of the righteous is a well of life," (Prov. 10:11). So what kind of words should we draw up from the well of life on a regular basis?

Say So

In God's kingdom, we have absolute freedom of speech. The psalmist told us, "Let the redeemed of the Lord say so" (Ps. 107:2). What should the redeemed say? We need to say what is so. As the redeemed, we need to declare the truth about who we are in Christ. We need to decree the redemptive realities that are ours. Are you redeemed? Start saying so. To give you a jumpstart, let's look up several passages of Scripture that reveal our redemptive rights.

Galatians 3—I Will Say So: Galatians 3:13 NIV says, "Christ redeemed us from the curse of the law by becoming a curse for us." It might sound something like this: "Jesus has redeemed me—spirit, soul and body—from the curse. I am the redeemed, and I say so. I am redeemed from sin and death unto life eternal. I am forgiven. I am alive. I am the righteousness of God in Christ. I am redeemed from sickness and disease unto health, wholeness and healing. I say so. All the systems of my body—my immune system, circulatory system, nervous system, muscular system, endocrine system, lymphatic system, reproductive system, skeletal system, cardiovascular system, digestive system, connective-tissue system and every other system—are strong and healthy. I am redeemed from poverty and lack unto abundance, increase and plenty. I am blessed to be a blessing. My God meets all my needs. I am the Lord's servant, and He takes pleasure in my prosperity. The blessing of the Lord makes me rich in every way. I am redeemed, and I say so!"

Psalm 91—I Will Say So: Psalm 91:2 says, "I will say of the Lord, 'He is my refuge and my fortress; my God, in him will I trust.'" If you struggle with fear and anxiety about your protection or the safety of your family, let these words fill your heart and mouth, "I will say of the Lord, He is my refuge. I declare, 'The name of Jesus and the blood of Jesus and the angels of God surround me and protect me everywhere I go, front to back, side to side, top to bottom, spirit, soul and body.' My trust is in the Lord."

Joel 3—I Will Say So: Joel 3:10 says, "Let the weak say, 'I am strong.'" God wants us to have grit. We need to declare our readiness for battle, our strengths and our victories. Somebody once asked me, "Yeah, but what if I don't feel strong? Isn't that lying?" No, there's a difference between reality and truth. Truth always trumps reality. Reality may say you're feeling weak, but the truth is you are strong in the Lord. So, let the

Truth always trumps reality.

weak say something. It's never a lie to speak the truth. Say it: "I am strong in the Lord and the power of His might. I'll say it again: I am strong in the Lord and the power of His might."

Psalm 112—I Will Say So: Psalm 112:1-3 NIV says, "Blessed is the man who fears the Lord, who finds great delight in his commands. His children will be mighty in the land; the generation of the upright will be blessed. Wealth and riches are in his house, and his righteousness endures forever."

You need to declare God's blessings over your family. You can and should say good things about your spouse, your kids and your finances: "My marriage is blessed. I love my wife/husband. We have a marriage made in heaven." What does that mean? It means your marriage is glued together by God's blessings.

Say, "My children are mighty in all the land." What does that mean? It means they're strong and stable. It means they're successful and influential.

Say, "Wealth and riches are in my house." What does that mean? It means God gives you wisdom, favor and opportunities to prosper.

Philippians 4—I Will Say So: Philippians 4:13 says, "I can do all things through Christ who strengthens me." Many people struggle with feelings of inferiority, intimidation and insecurity. If you are one of them, get God's Word in your heart and mouth.

God needs people who really believe they can do all things through Christ who strengthens them. The Lord needs people who can spin more than one plate without being overwhelmed. He needs people who can withstand a little pressure and tribulation and still come out swinging. God is looking for people willing to increase their capacity.

God is looking for people willing to increase their capacity.

If the Lord is ever going to reach the world with the gospel, He's going to do it through us—His people. In order to do that, He needs people who know how to work a job, raise a family and serve Him. The Lord can't ask us to do something and then hear us bellyache about how many hours it takes, have a meltdown because we are too tired or require counseling because we were asked to serve in church. The only way to do all God has called us to do is to tap into the truth that we can do all things through Christ who strengthens us.

Today, say this, "I can do all things through Christ who strengthens me. I can do everything the Lord asks me to do. By God's grace, wisdom and strength, I can do all things through Christ."

Say Something

Not only do we need to say "so", we need to say "something"! When we speak, we need to be brutally honest and ask ourselves, "Am I just talking or actually saying something?" "The words of a [discreet and wise] man's mouth are like deep waters [plenteous and difficult to fathom], and the fountain of skillful and godly Wisdom is like a gushing stream [sparkling, fresh, pure, and life-giving]," (Prov. 18:4 AMP).

Have you noticed there's a difference between words that carry weight and words that are void? Be the kind of person who speaks words that say something. A wise person speaks words that carry substance—"there's life in them there words"—words that have depth, words that minister grace to the hearers, words that impart life, words that encourage, words that teach, words that build up, words that comfort, words that get to the heart. Notice a wise person has plenty of deep words that want to gush like a stream. Wise people don't lack for deep words.

A fool just talks—"there's a hollowness to those words"—words that are vacant, words that are shallow, words that minister nothing, words that don't impart, words that discourage, words that are empty, words that never make it to the heart—they dissipate. A fool doesn't have much to say; his or her words are repetitive and nonsensical.

Which one are you? A wise person is known by his words . . . as is a fool. Jesus says, "For out of the abundance of the heart the mouth speaks," (Matt.12:34). If deep things fill our hearts (enriching things like God's Word, His wisdom, His knowledge, understanding, direction and divine revelation), then those are the deep waters that will come out of our mouths to bless those around us. It will just happen because we will speak out the things that are in our hearts in abundance.

If shallow things fill our hearts (uninteresting thoughts, TV, sports, the weather, the latest joke, gossip and trivia), then those are the shallow things that will come out of our mouths. Again, it will just happen because we will speak out the things that are in our hearts in abundance.

If you want to say something, have something to say. Fill your heart and mind with the Word of God, and be intentional about engaging in intelligent, stimulating, life-giving conversations that impart grace to all who hear.

Say What?

Make sure you say so, say something and pay attention to what you say. Here's why: we will be judged by our words.

The other day I was thinking about what it's going to be like to stand before the Lord. I was pondering the idea that God is a fair judge, and when He inspects our lives and we face His judgment, He will be completely fair to every single person—believer and unbeliever alike. While I was thinking about this, the Holy Spirit reminded me of this Scripture, "But I tell you, on the day of judgment men will have to give account for every idle (inoperative, nonworking) word they speak. For by your words you will be justified and acquitted, and by your words you will be condemned and sentenced," (Matt. 12:36,37 AMP). I was especially drawn to the phrase, "For by your words you will be justified and acquitted and by your words you will be condemned and sentenced." It hit me with soberness—how many of our words do we think are idle, inoperative and nonworking?

Words About God, Heaven and Hell: It occurred to me that there are many people who have said things like, "I don't believe in God. I don't believe in Jesus. I just want to go to hell to party with all my friends." At the judgment, God is required by His own Word to sentence them according to their words.

On the other hand, I thought about how many people have confessed these words from their hearts, "Jesus I surrender to You. I confess You as the Lord of my life, and I trust in Your shed blood for my salvation." How reassuring it is to know God is required by His own Word to acquit them. Our words will be our judge.

I talked with a man a few years ago who told me he didn't believe in God or Jesus, and then he asked me if he would go to heaven or hell. I told him according to the

Bible, God wouldn't send him to heaven or hell—his own words would send him to his final destination. He was shocked. I explained Jesus said we would be justified or condemned by our words. I tried to paint the scenario for him. I said, "When you stand before God, He will tell you the truth—Jesus is the way, the truth and the life; and no one comes to the Father except through Him. Then, God will play the tape of your words—the ones you just said to me about not believing in God or Jesus. God will be obligated, according to His own Word, to oblige your words; and according to your own words, you will be condemned."

Then this man said, "Well, I thought God would give me a break."

I responded, "I thought you didn't believe in God."

He smiled and said I had given him something to think about. I hope he did think about it, and I pray he had a change of heart and words.

Words About God, Life and Ourselves: As I pondered Jesus' words, I realized many times we are our own worst enemy—simply through the words we speak. How many times do we become frustrated, mad or about to give up because we don't understand why something happened or didn't happen? And just when we are ready to accuse God of not being fair, He will play the tape of our own words. We'll discover that the very things we said were the very things we got:

"Well, I didn't think all that faith stuff was going to work anyway."

"I am just scared to death things won't work out."

"God doesn't care about me."

"God has forgotten about me."

"I'll probably get sick."

"I bet I'll get fired."

"I am just sick and tired."

. . . and a host of other unbelieving statements we make.

God is obligated by His own Word to hold us accountable for our words. Our words will be our judge. A preacher friend of ours compares the words we say to the recording in the black box—the flight data recorder on an airplane. The black box records everything that is said in the cockpit. In the event of a disaster, the authorities can listen to the last words of those in a crash. I wonder what the black box of our lives sounds like? If we listened to the black box and heard the last words we said right before we "crashed," our eyes would be opened to an accurate picture of what went wrong and why God had to allow and/or permit certain things to happen or not happen. "For by your words you will be justified, and by your words you will be condemned," (Matt. 12:37).

CHAPTER 15:

Get Your Ask in Gear

We need help to get our ask in gear! The Bible is clear: the Lord wants us to ask Him for and about things. He does. It's interesting how many times the Bible tells us to ask. God likes it when we ask. While the Lord knows everything we have need of, He still likes to be asked.

Ask Nicely

James said something very interesting about asking, "You want what you don't have, so you scheme and kill to get it. You are jealous of what others have, but you can't get it, so you fight and wage war to take it away from them. Yet you don't have what you want because you don't ask God for it. And even when you ask, you don't get it because your motives are all wrong—you want only what will give you pleasure," (4:2,3 NLT).

One reason some people don't have what they want is because they haven't asked God for it. Instead, they operate out of their flesh—they scheme, kill, fight and quarrel—to obtain things, yet they still don't have what they want. Another reason some people don't get what they want is because when they finally decide to ask God for the things they desire, their motives are not in the right place. They want things for selfish reasons, not to bring Him praise or glory, and for that reason God cannot give them what they ask for.

As parents, we understand this. Have you ever observed a self-absorbed, whiney, spoiled child having a hissy fit while asking or demanding things from his/her mom or dad? It's not a pretty sight. The truth is, most parents want to bless their children, but they don't want to indulge children who are nasty or greedy in their asking. Our heavenly Father is telling us the same thing. He loves to give His children good gifts, but He doesn't want to indulge our selfish motives and carnal ambitions. He likes to be asked, and we need to ask nicely.

Don't assume or presume but ask.

Have you asked the Lord for anything lately? What type of attitude did you have? What were your motives? Did you ask nicely? God wants you to ask. Don't assume or presume but ask. When you ask the Lord from a heart of pure motivation, you can have great confidence He will hear and answer your words. (James 4:3.)

Look at what the Lord says about His desire to answer and our need to get busy asking.

Ask Anyway: Matthew 6:8—"For your Father knows the things you have need of before you ask Him." God knows what we need, but He still wants to be asked.

Ask and Receive Good Things: Matthew 7:7-11—"Ask, and it will be given to you; seek, and you will find; knock, and it will be opened to you. For everyone who asks receives, and he who seeks finds, and to him who knocks it will be opened. Or what man is there among you who, if his son asks for bread, will give him a stone? Or if he asks for a fish, will he give him a serpent? If you then, being evil, know how to give good gifts to your children, how much more will your Father who is in heaven give good things to those who ask Him!" The Lord promised great things for those who ask Him.

Ask and Agree: Matthew 18:19—"'Again I say to you that if two of you agree on earth concerning anything that they ask, it will be done for them by My Father in heaven.'" When two of us ask and agree, God promises to hear and answer.

Ask About Whatever: Matthew 21:22—"And whatever things you ask in prayer, believing, you will receive." If we believe God and His Word, we can ask about "whatever."

Ask in Jesus' Name: John 14:13-14—"And whatever you ask in My name, that I will do, that the Father may be glorified in the Son. If you ask anything in My name, I will do it." We can ask about anything in accordance with His Word and in His name.

Ask According to the Word: John 15:7—"If you abide in Me, and My words abide in you, you will ask what you desire, and it shall be done for you." When we abide in Him and His Word, He fills our hearts with His desires. When we ask for those desires, He will answer.

Ask and Receive Joy: John 16:23-24—"And in that day you will ask Me nothing. Most assuredly, I say to you, whatever you ask the Father in My name He will give you. Until now you have asked nothing in My name. Ask, and you will receive, that your joy may be full." When we ask and believe we receive, we will experience God's great joy.

Ask in Faith: James 1:5-6—"If any of you lacks wisdom, let him ask of God, who gives to all liberally and without reproach, and it will be given to him. But let him ask in faith, with no doubting, for he who doubts is like a wave of the sea driven and tossed by the wind." If we need wisdom, God will give it to us when we ask in faith.

When we ask God for anything in line with His Word and His will, He is eager to answer us.

Ask and Know: 1 John 5:14-15—"Now this is the confidence that we have in Him, that if we ask anything according to His will, He hears us. And if we know that He hears us, whatever we ask, we know that we have the petitions that we have asked of Him." When we ask for anything according to His will, we can be confident He hears us, and He will deliver.

It's remarkable how many times the Lord told us to ask! When we ask God for anything in line with His Word and His will, He is eager to answer us.

Set of Keys

Let's conclude this chapter with a set of keys. Jesus said,

"I will give you the keys of the kingdom of heaven; and whatever you bind (declare to be improper and unlawful) on earth must be what is already bound in heaven; and whatever you loose (declare lawful) on earth must be what is already loosed in heaven."

Matthew 16:19 AMP

Keys give us access to places. Without the proper key, a car won't start, a door will remain closed and a closet will be locked; but with the right keys, we have access to everything. Jesus gave us a pretty important set of keys. Through these keys, He's given us access to heaven's power and blessings.

With the right keys, we have access to everything.

The Bind Key: One vital key of the kingdom is the ability to bind—to declare things to be improper or unlawful.

The Loose Key: Another vital key is the ability to loose—to declare things to be lawful.

Jesus has given us authority to bind and loose. We have been authorized to use our voices to activate things in heaven and on earth. If we bind it on earth, heaven will reinforce it; if we loose it on earth, heaven will release it. As believers, the Lord wants us to exercise our faith to bind and loose things in our sphere of authority.

When we give voice to God's Word, God's plan and His authority, it sets His will into motion in our lives. One way to apply these keys is to say something similar to this: "In the name of Jesus, I bind the works of the devil in my life. I agree with heaven, and I bind and declare unlawful every demon and work of the enemy to steal, kill or destroy me or my family, business or ministry in any way. In Jesus' name, I loose the power of almighty God in my life. I agree with heaven, and I loose and declare lawful the power of His wisdom, His favor, His healing power and His goodness to work mightily in my life. In Jesus' name."

We know that heaven will back this confession of faith and this act of binding and loosing because all the works of the devil have been declared improper and unlawful by heaven. When we bind his works, we are agreeing with God. We know that the power of God's wisdom, favor, healing and goodness is lawful in heaven, so we can loose and declare that power in our lives on earth. When we loose God's power, we are voice activating His will.

Simple. Powerful. True.

If you haven't used your keys lately, go ahead and pull them out and get busy binding, loosing and asking God for things that are congruent with His will and His Word.

CHAPTER 16:

Big Talkers

Ever heard the phrase, "Big hat, no cattle"? You get the idea this cowboy's wearing a big hat to impress people, but if anyone looked behind the façade, they'd notice there are no cattle on his ranch. He may be a big talker and full of hot air, but there's no substance to back him up.

God doesn't want us to be full of hot air. He wants us to be big talkers whose words are weighty, powerful and full of faith and life-giving substance. The writer of Proverbs said, "The mouth of the righteous is a fountain of life," (10:11 NIV).

Let's conclude this book by looking at a few more ways to be big talkers whose words are a fountain of life.

A Big Shout

Do you want to tap into the river of joy, happiness and laughter in a greater way? Shout for it! That's right—open up your mouth and start shouting. The Bible tells us to do it. We should shout for joy and victory.

> "But let all those rejoice who put their trust in You; let them ever shout for joy, because You defend them; let those also who love Your name be joyful in You."
>
> Psalm 5:11

> "Be glad in the Lord and rejoice, you righteous; and shout for joy, all you upright in heart!"
>
> Psalm 32:11

> "Let them shout for joy and be glad, who favor my righteous cause; and let them say continually, 'Let the Lord be magnified, who has pleasure in the prosperity of His servant.' And my tongue shall speak of Your righteousness and of Your praise all the day long."
>
> Psalm 35:27-28

> "Oh, clap your hands, all you peoples! Shout to God with the voice of triumph!"
>
> Psalm 47:1

Why not get alone with the Lord and start shouting? It might sound like this:

"I shout for joy! Woo hoo! (Jump up and down.) I am not going to be depressed or down in the dumps. The joy of the Lord is my strength—I shout for joy! I shout to God with a voice of triumph! Joy, I am shouting for you! I shout for joy! Hallelujah! Praise the Lord! Glory to God! The joy of the Lord fills my life. Woo hoo!" (Continue jumping and shouting until joy kicks in.)

Sing A Big Song

Maybe you have a need to get intoxicated with the Spirit and live under the influence of His joy and peace. The Lord has provided a way: sing a song.

> And do not be drunk with wine, in which is dissipation; but be filled with the Spirit, speaking to one another in psalms and hymns and spiritual songs, singing and making melody in your heart to the Lord, giving thanks always for all things to God the Father in the name of our Lord Jesus Christ.
>
> Ephesians 5:18-20

We need to fill our mouths with songs and melodies. Have God-songs filled your heart and mouth lately? They should. If you've been singing the blues, or if you've lost your song, you can get it back. Don't quit singing. Just change your tune. Bust out and start singing again.

There is something fun and refreshing about being intoxicated with the Spirit and living under the influence of His power. The way we get there is by speaking and singing. It's easy to do. To get started, play some of your favorite worship music and spend some time thanking, praising and worshipping the Lord. Then turn the music off, and listen to the melody God puts in your heart. When you do, you'll find a tune, word, phrase or theme bubbling up from your heart. Sing it out. Even if you're not on pitch or your words don't rhyme, it's still music to God's ears.

I've practiced this type of thing in my own private walk with the Lord for many, many years, and it's one of the most spiritually refreshing things I've experienced. When we release the rivers of living water in our hearts through singing and making a melody to the Lord, His presence splashes on us, and we are refreshed.

Years ago as I was driving to Chicago, the Lord put this song in my heart, and I sang it out in the car. It turned out to be an exhortation to get a grip on our lip.

God Has a Word for the Weary

God has a word for the weary,
God has a word for the weak.
This is His Word are you listening?
His word is simply: Speak!

Don't be silent, don't be silent,
Don't doubt, don't pout.
Don't be silent,
Don't you doubt, and don't you pout.

But let the weak speak,
Let the weak speak.

Let the weak say, "I am strong."
God is not wrong.

Let the weak and the weary,
Let them not become bleary.
But let them speak,
And sing the Word.

Sing the Word,
Sing the Word.
Declare what you know.
And you'll find, God is with you,
From your heart as you go.

Sing it out,
Sing it out.
Sing it loud,
Sing it strong.

You may not even know what to say,
But that's okay.
The words will come,
Just speak and sing it now.

God has a word for the weary,
God has a word for the weak.
This is His Word are you listening?
His word is simply: Speak!
Are you ready to be a doer of the Word?
Speak! Shout! Sing!

Go for it! You'll tap into a whole new realm of joy and refreshing: "The Lord is my strength and my shield; my heart trusted in him, and I am helped: therefore my heart greatly rejoiceth; and with my song will I praise him," (Ps. 28:7 KJV).

Big Words

Big words—God wants to fill our mouths with His Word, especially big words that honor and glorify Him. So, let's truly get a grip on our lip as we talk with our mouth full of His big words. Be a big talker. Talk about how big God is. Magnify Him, and exalt His name. He's a big God, and He's given us some big words to believe: "Ah, Lord God! Behold, You have made the heavens and the earth by Your great power and outstretched arm. There is nothing too hard for You," (Jer. 32:17).

Five words can revolutionize your eternity, your mind, your body, your family, your future and every part of your life. These big, life-changing words are:

Whoever

Anything

Whatever

All Things

Always.

Whoever: "For God so loved the world that He gave His only begotten Son, that WHOEVER believes in Him should not perish but have everlasting life," (John 3:16, emphasis mine).

Aren't you glad that eternal life is open to whomever? Eternal life isn't just for a select few—it's for whoever believes on Jesus. Your name, age, size, ethnicity, language, religious background or gender makes no difference. If you are a whoever, you qualify for eternal life by believing in Jesus. *Say it: I am a whoever!*

Anything: "Behold, I am the Lord, the God of all flesh. Is there ANYTHING too hard for Me?" (Jer. 32:27, emphasis mine).

God can handle anything you are facing. Nothing is too hard for our almighty, all-powerful God. If we will put our complete trust Him, there isn't anything He can't fix, cure, forgive, stabilize, heal or bless. Is anything too hard for God? Not one thing. *Say it: God can do anything!*

Whatever: "For assuredly, I say to you, whoever says to this mountain, 'Be removed and be cast into the sea,' and does not doubt in his heart, but believes that those things he says will be done, he will have WHATEVER he says," (Mark 11:23, emphasis mine).

If we will get our hearts and mouths in agreement with God and His Word, it's absolutely true we can have whatever we say. Mmm . . . now, that's a big word. *Say it: I thank You, Lord, for all the whatevers!*

All Things: "For with God ALL THINGS are possible," (Mark 10:27, emphasis mine).

What is possible? All things. What do you need? It's possible. Yes, it is. All things you need are possible with God. Without God, you're on your own; but with God, all things are possible. *Say it: With God all things are possible in my life!*

Always: "Now thanks be to God who ALWAYS leads us in triumph in Christ, and through us diffuses the fragrance of His knowledge in every place," (2 Cor. 2:14, emphasis mine).

Does it get any bigger than always? God promises no matter how dark it may look, no matter how defeated you may feel, no matter what, He always leads you in triumph in Christ. Get a vision of victory in your mind and heart today. Fix your eyes on that vision of triumph, and do not be moved. He always leads you to victory. *Say it: My God always causes me to triumph in Christ!*

Final Words

Ta-da! I hope you have been inspired and challenged through *Get a Grip on Your Lip*.

As you close the cover of this book, I pray you will do these three things:

1. Reread it: Prayerfully read and reread this book often.

2. See it: Look up and meditate on each of the Scriptures in this book.

3. Do it: Be a doer of the word and put these things into practice.

I have no doubt that as you get a grip on your lip, God will do great things in and through you, and your life will never be the same.

> From the fruit of his mouth a man's stomach is filled; with the harvest from his lips he is satisfied. The tongue has the power of life and death, and those who love it will eat its fruit.
>
> Proverbs 18:20-21 NIV

Fifty Faith Confessions to Get a Grip on Your Lip

PRAISE AND THANKS

This is the day that the Lord has made, and I will rejoice and be glad in it. The Lord is good and His mercy endures forever. Today, I will taste and see that the Lord is good. (Ps. 118:124; Ps. 34:8.)

I will bless the Lord, and His praise will continually be in my mouth. Bless the Lord, oh my soul, and forget not all His benefits. I bless the Lord—I thank You, Father, for Your mercies that are new every morning. Great is Your faithfulness. I praise You Jesus for being my Lord and Savior. I bless You Holy Spirit for being the Greater One who lives in me. Today, I bless the Lord—Father, Son and Holy Spirit. (Ps. 34:1; Ps. 103:3; Lam. 3:23; Phil. 2:11; 1 John 4:4.)

I give thanks with a grateful heart. The Lord has been good to me. I rejoice in the Lord always. I shout for joy. I lift up my hands in Your Name. I sing songs of praise. Today, I put on the garment of praise and thanks. (Ps. 136; Ps. 150; Ps. 32:11; Isa. 61:3.)

I praise You, Lord, for what You have done for me. Jesus, You were wounded and crushed for my sins. You were beaten that I might have peace. You were whipped, and I was healed. You have blessed me with forgiveness, righteousness, favor, grace, peace, wisdom, knowledge, healing and good things. I worship You for who You are— You are my Lord, Savior, Redeemer, Healer, Restorer, Helper and Good Shepherd. Today, I praise and worship You in Spirit and truth. (Isa. 53:5; John 4:24.)

I enter Your courts with thanksgiving in my heart. I enter Your courts with praise. I come before Your Presence with singing. In Your Presence is fullness of joy. Today, I give you my thanks, praise and singing. (Ps. 100.)

SALVATION AND REDEMPTION

I am saved. I am a child of God. God is my Father. Jesus is the Lord of my life. The Holy Spirit is my Helper. Today, I say I am saved. (Rom. 10:8,9; 13.)

I am the redeemed, so I say so. Because of Jesus, I say I am redeemed from sin and death to eternal life. I am redeemed from poverty and lack to abundance and prosperity. I am redeemed from sickness and disease to health, healing and wholeness. Today, I say I am Redeemed. (Ps. 107:2; Gal. 3:13.)

I have been made the righteousness of God in Christ. The blood of Jesus cleanses me from all sin, and I have been made as righteous as God Himself through Christ. Therefore, I am free from any sense of guilt, inferiority or unworthiness. Because of Jesus, I have been made worthy and righteous. Today, I say I am the righteousness of God in Christ. (2 Cor. 5:21.)

I have been redeemed from the curse of the law. I have been set free from my past. I have been saved from sin and darkness. I have been rescued from a life of emptiness, guilt, disillusionment and distress. Today, I am a born-again Christian and full of the life of God, the love of God, the Word of God and the blessings of God. (Deut. 28; Gal. 3:13.)

I have been bought with a price, and I am not my own. I belong to Jesus. I am redeemed, saved and sanctified. Today, I say I am a blood-bought, Spirit-taught,

Bible-loving, devil-chasing, hell-rescuing, heaven-bound, on-fire, born-again, unashamed believer, follower, servant, worshipper and friend of the Lord Jesus Christ. (1 Cor. 6:20.)

HEALING

By Jesus' stripes, I am healed. Today, I call my body healed, healthy and whole. (1 Peter 2:24.)

He forgives all my sins and heals all my diseases. Today, I thank You, Lord, for forgiving all my sins and for Your healing power at work in my body driving out all diseases. (Ps. 103:3.)

He blesses my bread and water and takes sickness away from the midst of me. He is the Lord that heals me. Today, I declare You are the God that heals me. (Ex. 23:25.)

Jesus of Nazareth was anointed with the Holy Spirit and power, and He went about doing good and healing all who were oppressed of the devil because God was with Him. Today, I declare in my life Jesus of Nazareth who is anointed with the Holy Spirit and power is doing good, healing me and setting me free from any oppression of the devil because God is with Him. (Acts 10:38.)

My Jesus is the same yesterday, today and forever. Yesterday, He healed all who came to Him; and today, I believe He is my Healer and Great Physician. Today, I call every system, tissue, fiber and cell of my body healed, healthy and whole. (Heb. 13:8.)

PROSPERITY AND ABUNDANCE

Jesus came to give us life and life more abundantly. Today, I declare the Lord's abundance in my life in every area—spirit, soul and body. (John 10:10.)

A generous person devises generous things, and by his generosity, he shall stand. Today, I am a generous person. I devise generous ways to bless others, and by my generosity, I will stand and stand out. (Isa. 32:8.)

The Holy Spirit prayed I would prosper and be in health even as my soul prospers. So, today I decree my soul prospers—my mind, will and emotions are in line with God's will and Word; therefore, I am prosperous and in health in every way. (3 John 2.)

God's favor surrounds me like a shield. Today, I have favor with everyone everywhere I go. God opens doors for me. The Lord gives me preferential treatment and loads me with benefits. All of His paths drip with abundance. Today, I declare I am blessed to be a blessing. (Ps. 5:12; Ps. 68:19; Ps. 65:11.)

The Lord takes pleasure in my prosperity. The blessing of the Lord makes me rich, and He adds no sorrow to it. Every good and perfect gift comes down from my Father in heaven, and He delights to give me good gifts. Today, I declare that I am blessed and highly favored. (Ps. 35:27; Prov. 10:22; James 1:17; Matt. 7:11.)

SPIRITUAL, MENTAL AND EMOTIONAL VICTORY

I am strong in the Lord and the power of His might. I put on the whole armor of God, and I enforce Satan's defeat in my life. No weapon formed against me shall prosper. Every tongue that rises against me in judgment, I will refute. I can do all things through Christ who strengthens me. Today, I am strong in the Lord. (Eph. 6:10-18; Isa. 54:17; Phil. 3:13.)

I have been raised up and seated with Christ. I am an heir of God and a co-heir with Christ. I have been given authority to use the name of Jesus—the name above every name. God has given me the victory through my Lord Jesus Christ. I am more than a conqueror through Christ, and He always leads me in triumph. I am an overcomer through my faith. Today, I am living on the victory side. (Eph. 2:6; Gal. 4:7; Phil. 2:9,10; 1 Cor. 15:57; Rom. 8:37; 2 Cor. 2:14; 1 John 5:4.)

I keep my mind stayed on Jesus and His Word, and the Lord keeps me in perfect peace. Today, I fix my mind and heart on Jesus, and I live in perfect peace. (Isa. 26:3.)

God has not given me a spirit of fear but a spirit of power, love and a sound mind. I am not anxious for anything, but in everything I give my cares and prayers to the Lord, and He guards my mind and heart in the peace that passes all understanding. Today, I am free to live in joy and peace. (2 Tim. 1:7; Phil. 4:6-8.)

I rejoice in the Lord today. I am free from the spirit of heaviness, dread, depression and discouragement. I encourage myself in the Lord, and I rejoice because I know the Lord is on my side. If God is for me, who can be against me? Today, I declare the Lord is on my side, and I rejoice. (Phil. 4:4; Isa. 61:3; 1 Sam. 30:6; Ps. 118:6; Rom. 8:31.)

MARRIAGE AND FAMILY

What the Lord has joined together; let no one separate. Therefore, I will not allow separation, division, disunity or disharmony into my marriage through my thoughts, emotions or conversations. Today, I decree the Lord has given me a marriage made in heaven. (Matt. 19:6.)

A house united will stand strong. My spouse and I will be in agreement, and with one mind and one mouth we will glorify the Lord and live a life fully pleasing to Him in every area of our lives spirit, soul and body. Today, I decree our family is united and strong. (Mark 3:24,25; Rom. 15:5-7.)

As for me and my house, we will serve the Lord. Our family is blessed. Our children are mighty in the Lord and mightily used of God. Today, I say we are a family of influence and destiny. (Josh. 24:15; Ps. 112.)

We train up our kids in the ways of the Lord—with God's wisdom and grace—and when they are old, they will not depart from it. Our kids will walk in the light of God's Word. They are taught by the Lord. They are full of great peace. Terror and fear are far from them. Today, I declare our kids are taught of the Lord, and He speaks to them day and night. (Prov. 22:6; Isa. 54:13,14.)

I am raising a generation that seeks, praises and obeys the Lord, a generation that knows and loves God and His Word and passes it on to future generations. Today, I say I will serve my generation and the generations ahead of

and behind me with the Gospel of Jesus Christ. (Ps. 24:6;
78:6-8; Acts 13:36.)

RELATIONSHIPS

God's love is the best way to build relationships. Today, I say according to 1 Corinthians 13, I walk in God's love, endure long and am patient and kind; I am never envious nor boiling over with jealousy; I am not boastful or vainglorious; I do not display myself haughtily. I am not conceited (arrogant and inflated with pride); I am not rude (unmannerly) and do not act unbecomingly. I (with God's love in me) do not insist on my own rights or my own way, for I am not self-seeking; I am not touchy or fretful or resentful; I take no account of the evil done to me, and I pay no attention to a suffered wrong. I do not rejoice at injustice and unrighteousness, but I rejoice when right and truth prevail. I bear up under anything and everything that comes; I am ever ready to believe the best of every person; my hopes are fadeless under all circumstances, and I endure everything without weakening. God's love in me will never fail, never fade out or become obsolete or come to an end. (1 Cor. 13:4-8.)

I want to have friends, so I will show myself to be friendly. Today, I will sow friendship seeds. (Prov. 18:24.) I will consider the "one anothers" in my life. Today, I will greet, love, pray for, serve, receive, forbear, forgive, comfort, teach and admonish, edify, exhort and provoke to love and good deeds the others in my life. (Gal. 5:13.)

Your love covers a multitude of sins, and Your mercy removes them as far as the east is from the west. Today, I walk in Your love and mercy, and I forgive anyone for anything they have ever said or done to me. (Prov. 10:12; Ps. 103:12; Mark 11:25.)

I have the power to be a witness for the Lord. I am an ambassador for Christ. I am blessed to be a blessing. Today, I am on the lookout for ways to share the Gospel of Jesus Christ, the love of God and His life and light with others. (Acts 1:8; 2 Cor. 5:20; Matt. 5:16.)

CAREER AND VOCATION

God's gifts and callings are without repentance, and He has a plan and a purpose for my life. He has created me as His workmanship and prepared me to walk in good works. Today, I decree I will find and fulfill God's gifts, callings and good works. (Rom. 11:29; Eph. 2:10.)

The Lord wants me to stand perfect and complete in His will. I believe the Lord is opening the eyes of my heart so I can know the hope of His calling in my life. Today, I agree with God, and by His grace, I will stand perfect and complete in all of His will. (Col. 4:12; Eph. 1:18.)

Jesus is the Lord of my life and my job and vocation. I know any successful enterprise is built by wise planning, common sense and staying abreast of the facts. Today, I declare the Lord guides me with wisdom, common sense and godly counsel. (Prov. 24:3; 15:22.)

The Lord is the Creator of the ends of the earth, and all knowledge and wisdom come from Him. He freely gives wisdom to all who ask. Today, I say the Holy Spirit gives me the wisdom I need in my line of work, my job and vocation. He shows me things to come; He gives me knowledge of witty inventions, and He gives me the innovative edge in all I do to honor Him. (James 1:5; John 16:13; Prov. 8:12.)

I work heartily as unto the Lord. I don't work to please men but to please the Lord. I know the Lord will reward me. Today, I work for an Audience of One. (Col. 3:22,24.)

MINISTRY AND CALLING

I did not choose the Lord: He chose me and ordained I should bear much fruit—fruit that remains. Today, I decree I will fulfill my God-given purpose to bear fruit, much fruit and fruit that remains to glorify the Lord for all eternity. (John 15:16.)

The Lord gave gifts to His people for the building up of His Body. I will be a wise steward of the gifts He has given to me. I will use and maximize the gifts He has given me for His purposes and His glory. I am a wise and faithful servant. I will be a wise steward and faithful in everything. When I am faithful in another person's ministry, the Lord will give me my own ministry. When the Lord counts me faithful, He will promote me in ministry. Today, I declare I am a wise and faithful steward. (Eph. 4:11-16; Matt. 24:25,26; Luke 16:10-12; 1 Tim. 1:12.)

I will not build on the foundation of Jesus Christ in my life with wood, hay or stubble; but I will build upon that foundation with gold, silver and precious stones. Today, I will invest my life not in temporary things that are seen but in eternal things that are unseen. (1 Cor. 3:11-15; 4:17,18.)

There is a divinely implanted sense of purpose in my heart and life. Nothing under the sun can satisfy me until I am walking in and fulfilling my divine purpose. Today, I say the Lord is ordering my steps to find and fulfill His divine purpose for my life. (Eccl. 3:11.)

Jesus is the Alpha and the Omega. Jesus is the Author and Finisher. Jesus began a good work in me, and He will bring it to completion. Today, I declare I will keep my eyes on Jesus, and I will run my race and finish my course with joy. (Rev. 1:8; Heb. 12:1,2; Phil. 1:6; 2:16; Acts 20:24.)

THE CHURCH

Jesus is building His church, and the gates of hell shall not prevail against it. The church of the Lord Jesus Christ is front and center in God's purposes. Jesus is the Head, and we are His Body. Today, I declare His church is alive and well; indeed, Jesus is building His church around the world. (Matt. 16:18.)

Jesus is the Chief Shepherd, and He has delegated authority and given gifts to those He has called to pioneer, plant, pastor and lead His church. He has given us shepherds after His own heart who shall feed us with knowledge and understanding. Today, I declare my pastor and church leaders are shepherds after God's own heart; they are called, anointed, strengthened and blessed by God to lead His church and accomplish His purpose. (1 Pet. 5:4; Jer. 3:15.)

It's good and pleasant when brothers and sisters dwell together in unity, for in that place, the Lord commands His blessing. Today, I declare my church is a place of unity, and the Lord commands His blessing on my church. (Ps. 133.)

In the last days, God will pour out His Spirit on all flesh, and our sons and daughters will prophesy; our young men will see visions; and our old men will dream dreams. Today, I agree with God's Word that we are living in the last days, and He is pouring out His Spirit on all flesh. (Acts 2:17,18.)

Jesus will return for a glorious church without spot or wrinkle. Today, I say I am a part of that glorious church; come quickly Lord Jesus. (Eph. 5:27; Rev. 1:7; 22.)

ABOUT THE AUTHOR

Beth Jones is a Bible teacher, author, wife and mother of four children, who ministers the Word in a relevant, humorous and inspiring way by sharing down-to-earth insights. She is the author of the popular *Getting a Grip on the Basics* series, which is being used by thousands of churches in America and abroad and has been translated into over a dozen languages. She's the author of *Jump Start 365*, a book of daily devos to start your day with God and over a dozen other books. She also writes the free, daily Jump Start Daily eDevo for over 5000 subscribers.

Beth and her husband Jeff founded and serve as the senior pastors of the growing Valley Family Church in Kalamazoo, Michigan.

For more information, please visit www.bethjones.org and www.valleyfamilychurch.org.